Crafting

Opinion and Persuasive Papers

Crafting
Opinion and Persuasive Papers

Tim Clifford

 Maupin House by
capstone
professional

Crafting Opinion and Persuasive Papers
by Tim Clifford

Cover and Book Design: Hank McAfee
Layout: Mickey Cuthbertson

Library of Congress Cataloging-in-Publication Data

Clifford, Tim, 1959-
 Crafting opinion and persuasive papers / by Tim Clifford.
   p. cm.
 Includes bibliographical references.
 ISBN 978-0-929895-61-1 (pbk.)
 1. English language--Composition and exercises--Study and teaching
(Elementary) 2. Language arts (Elementary) 3. Persuasion (Rhetoric)-
-Study and teaching (Elementary) 4. English language--Composition
and exercises--Study and teaching (Secondary) 5. Language arts
(Secondary) 6. Persuasion (Rhetoric)--Study and teaching (Secondary)
I. Title.
LB1576.C5654 2007
372.62'3--dc22
                              2007018655

ISBN-10: 0-929895-61-4
ISBN-13: 978-0-929895-61-1

Maupin House by
capstone professional

Maupin House Publishing, Inc. by Capstone Professional
1710 Roe Crest Drive
North Mankato, MN 56003

888-262-6135
www.capstoneclassroom.com

Publishing Professional Resources that Improve Classroom Performance

Printed in the United States of America in Eau Claire, Wisconsin.
052014 008255

To the women in my life, past and present, including my wife Danna, my daughters Meg and Katey, my mother Katherine, and my mother-in-law Louise. Each of them has persuaded me to do many things in my life, often against my better judgment. Naturally, they were almost always right.

CONTENTS

CONTENTS (continued)

Acknowledgements

Many thanks to Marcia S. Freeman, who gave generously of her time to review my efforts in writing this book. Her insights and expertise are greatly appreciated.

CHAPTER 1

Introduction to Teaching Opinion and Persuasive Writing

› Why Teach Opinion and Persuasion?

Everyone has opinions, and everyone wants to talk about them. The proliferation of blogs and personal web spaces demonstrates how keenly people want their voices to be heard. Yet, while everyone has opinions, not everyone knows how to express them effectively or how to use them to persuade others. Teaching your students the craft of persuasion gives them the tools they need to make themselves heard and, more importantly, to get a fair hearing.

Teaching students how to write opinion and persuasive papers is essential because it incorporates a number of critical thinking and writing skills. Some of the more important skills your students need as they undertake opinion and persuasive writing include

- Understanding fact vs. opinion
- Supporting claims with evidence
- Logical organization and structure
- Comparison
- Understanding audience and author's purpose
- Using quotes and statistics
- Examining the validity of claims
- Precise word choice

In addition to helping students gain these skills, instruction in the craft of writing opinion and persuasive pieces encourages deep thinking about a subject. Knowing that Neil Armstrong landed on the moon in 1969 is important, but being able to evaluate whether the space program should be publicly or privately funded requires an altogether different and more complex thought process. Teaching your students how to make and effectively support such judgments will elevate them to some of the highest level thinking and writing they will do in their school careers.

Young people today are bombarded by messages intended to persuade them, from TV ads to political messages and everything in between. Understanding persuasion will enable your students to make better judgments about which messages are sound and which are specious.

› Defining Opinion and Persuasion

While related, opinion and persuasion are actually quite different. You can offer an opinion without being persuasive, but you can't persuade without offering an opinion.

When I teach these skills to my students, I often tell them that as a writer, "Opinion is about me, and persuasion is about you." I explain to them that when I write an opinion paper, I discuss what I think—my preferences, ideas, goals, and so forth. My purpose is to talk about me. In a persuasive paper, I'll do some of the same things, but I'll also have an additional purpose: to get you, the audience, to agree with me. This additional purpose adds a layer of complexity to persuasion that is lacking in opinion pieces. For this reason, opinion is generally taught in the earlier grades or as a precursor to persuasion.

> When Is Opinion and Persuasive Writing Taught?

Writing about opinions can begin as soon as students have opinions to express. Even the youngest writers can express preferences for certain books, foods, music, and so on. So, in a sense, it's never too early to start teaching children about opinion papers. Formally, however, most schools begin asking for such pieces to be included in student portfolios around third or fourth grade. Persuasive papers, being somewhat more complex, often are not required until later grades, but there's technically no good reason not to teach persuasion to students who understand opinion writing.

Depending on the level of your class or your own educational objectives for your students, you may choose to:

- Teach only opinion papers.
- Teach only persuasive essays.
- Teach opinion papers first and then build on those skills for persuasive essays.

There is no "right" way. Only you can determine what works best for your students. This book will help you no matter what you decide.

> Who Teaches Opinion and Persuasive Writing?

While English teachers have traditionally taught opinion and persuasion, it makes sense for other content-area teachers to join in. Content-area teachers can work in collaboration with English teachers by assigning topics that lend themselves to persuasive writing, or they can assign such topics themselves.

I firmly believe that content-area teachers should be teachers of writing as well. Who better to help students write a persuasive piece on a political candidate than a social studies teacher? Why shouldn't science teachers help students write papers advocating funding for space exploration? Teachers with specialized content knowledge can pinpoint the arguments that need to be made, and thus help students create effective opinion and persuasive papers.

This book contains all the tools you will need to teach opinion and persuasion, regardless of your content area. The lessons in this book teach explicit writing-craft skills that will help you transform your students into the writers they can be.

˃ The Instructional Sequence

The instructional sequence for opinion and persuasive writing is composed of four steps:

- **Step One—Identifying Issues** starts with understanding fact vs. opinion. From there, students learn how to choose, narrow, and research topics. At the end of this first step, students will write a proposal letter to you, asking permission to write about the topic they have chosen. I have provided a sample letter and a mini-rubric to assist students in this project. These letters will help you decide whether students have a sufficient grasp of the skills necessary to move on to Step Two.

- **Step Two—Crafting an Opinion Paper** takes students through the process of writing their opinion papers, from developing a thesis to writing all the paragraph types that will appear in the opinion paper. The goal this time is to write a fully developed opinion paper. A sheet of expectations and a rubric are included for evaluation purposes.

- **Step Three—Adding Persuasive Elements** shows students what they need to understand in order to transform their opinion papers into persuasive essays. The focus is on audience, author's purpose, and identifying relevant evidence for both sides of the issue. This step will help your students understand the differences between opinion and persuasion, and will prepare them for the more complex task of putting together their persuasive essays.

- **Step Four—Crafting a Persuasive Essay** zeroes in on the Target Skills® needed to persuade the reader, with an emphasis on organization and paragraph types.

Each of these steps is covered in its own chapter. Each step builds upon the previous, scaffolding necessary skills until your students can build effective essays based upon their mastery of each lesson.

˃ Before You Begin

Each student should have a writing notebook with a section devoted to opinion and persuasive writing. Many of the writing assignments will be done in this notebook, and you should encourage students to refer back to their earlier work as they continue to build their skills. In addition, each student should have a folder to store the many organizers and handouts they will use as they work through each step.

Most of the lessons in this book assume that your students are working in groups. Groups of four or five students usually work well. Smaller groups may not have enough work to share, and larger groups may require more than the allotted time to give everyone an opportunity to share. When students are asked to work with partners, it is so noted in the lesson.

It's probably a good idea to create groups that will work together throughout the unit; this gives students a familiarity with each other's topics that is generally beneficial.

It is crucial to model good writing for your class, and all of the writing lessons here contain some sort of writing sample for you to use with your students. For the reading lessons, however, you will need to gather opinion and persuasive articles. These can come from student magazines, the editorial section of mainstream news magazines, and the op-ed pages of local and national newspapers. Because you will need articles on a wide variety of topics, it's a good idea to ask students to begin gathering these reading materials for class use at least a week in advance of starting the first instructional block. School librarians can often be of great help by finding age-appropriate material for you to use. The Internet is a great resource as well. Online news sources may contain persuasive articles you can print for classroom use.

> What Does an Instructional Block Schedule Look Like?

In the introductory section for each instructional step, you will find a chart like the one below (taken from *Step Two—Crafting an Opinion Paper*).

Day	Lesson Name	Description
Day 1: Reading	Identifying Thesis Statements	Students will read Op-Ed pieces and magazine articles to find the thesis statement.
Day 1: Writing	Writing a Thesis Statement	Students will write a *for* or *against* statement that will form the thesis of their opinion paper.
Day 2: Reading	Identifying Support	Students will read to find the facts, quotes, and pictures used to support a thesis in an article.
Day 2: Writing	Supporting a Thesis	Students will create a graphic organizer of facts, quotes, and pictures that support the thesis of their opinion paper.

The chart shows you the recommended order of the instructional block. It assumes that you have a reading and writing period each day; if you do not, you will need to adjust the schedule accordingly. The optional lesson ideas that appear at the end of each chapter are not included in these charts, so you may wish to adjust the schedule to include any of those lessons that you wish to teach.

> The Lessons

Each step contains a number of essential lessons followed by a group of shorter optional lessons ideas. You should teach all of the essential lessons—they are the necessary parts of all opinion and persuasive papers. Some of the optional lessons supplement the essential lessons, while others teach new skills. Use the optional lessons ideas for enrichment or as needed to reinforce the essential skills.

Each essential lesson contains the following elements:

- **Why Teach It:** This section explains why the lesson is an essential one and how it will enhance your students' writing.
- **Materials Needed:** This tells you what handouts, transparencies, charts, or other materials you will need to teach the lesson.
- **Opening the Lesson:** Use this brief introduction to tell your class what you will be working on for the day and to set expectations for the lesson.
- **Modeling the Skill:** Each writing lesson calls for you to model a skill for your students. This section contains a suggested model that you may use for that purpose.
- **Work Time:** After you have modeled the skill, students begin working on practicing the skill themselves either on a reproducible handout or in their writer's notebook.

- **Closing Activity:** It is important for your students to share their work in order to receive feedback and to see how others have completed the task. Each closing activity gives your students an opportunity to assess their work for the day.

> The WHAM Mini-Lesson Format

If you read *The Middle School Writing Toolkit: Differentiated Instruction across the Content Areas* (Maupin House, 2007), my previous book on writer's craft, then you should already be familiar with the WHAM mini-lesson format. If not, here's a crash course that you may wish to use when teaching the lessons in this book.

WHAM stands for Watch, Help, Apply, and Master, a four-step approach to teaching Target Skills®:

- **WATCH**: Students watch the teacher perform the skill.
- **HELP:** Students help the teacher perform the skill using a different example.
- **APPLY:** Students apply the skill by working on a few brief examples as the teacher assists.
- **MASTER:** Students work on mastering the skill during their work time.

As I explained on page 6 of *The Middle School Writing Toolkit*, the WHAM format echoes the "I do, you watch" gradual release of responsibility model advanced by Jeffrey Wilhelm in *Strategic Reading* (Heinemann, 2001). It adds the advantage of creating terminology that teachers and students can share—when I tell students we're going to "WHAM" a skill, they know the steps we are going to take.

Each mini-lesson should last from ten to fifteen minutes. Ideally, each part of the process should last for about three or four minutes. Of course, if you are introducing a new skill to students, you may have to spend more time modeling the skill early in the mini-lesson. For skills that are mostly review or practice, you may wish to adjust your timing for less modeling and more application of the skill.

Here's a walkthrough of how you might WHAM Understanding Fact vs. Opinion, the first lesson in this book (see page 11). Here is part one of the reproducible for that lesson:

TOPIC	FACT	OPINION
Sports	My team has 27 wins and only 4 losses.	My team is the best team in the league!
Education		Math is my favorite subject.
Science	The sun is 93 million miles from Earth.	
History		The Civil War was the worst war in US history.
Math	2+2=4	
Music		Beethoven was a great composer.

For the **WATCH** part of the lesson, you would introduce the skill and do the first entry for the class, explaining for the "Sports" topic why "My team has 27 wins and only 4 losses" is a fact and why "My team is the best team in the league!" is an opinion.

For the **HELP** part, you would ask students to help you fill in the blanks for the "Education" and "Science" topics.

For the **APPLY** part, students would complete the rows for the remaining three topics themselves as you circulate the room and check comprehension.

Finally, for the **MASTER** part, you would use Part Two of the handout and ask students to complete it on their own:

> Create a page in your writer's notebook called "Fact vs. Opinion." Create a table like the one above and record at least five opinions and five facts. You may use whatever topics you wish in the "Topics" column.

Structuring a lesson in this way gives your students increasing responsibility at each step. It also gives you a way to gauge their comprehension along the way.

> Using CraftPlus®

Although this book can be used on its own, it is also designed to be a Supplemental Resource for CraftPlus®. If you are unfamiliar with CraftPlus®, it is a set of principles and practices for teaching explicit writing skills (called Target Skills®) to students.

CraftPlus was developed by developed by Marcia Freeman. In the Appendix of this book (see page 108), you will find an overview of CraftPlus taken from Susan Koehler's excellent book, *Crafting Expository Papers*. I am indebted to her for allowing me to reproduce it here.

CHAPTER 2
Step One—Identifying Issues

Opinion and persuasion are everywhere.

Turn on the television, browse the Internet, or flip the pages of a magazine and you'll see countless examples of advertisements in which companies offer their opinions of their products and try to persuade us to buy them. News shows and editorial pages try to convince us of the validity of their points of view. Even reality shows try to sway us into voting for certain contestants.

Still, with all this in front of them on a daily basis, your students may have trouble identifying issues they want to write about for their opinion and persuasive papers. It is crucial, therefore, that you take as much time as your students need to explore, identify, and choose issues to write about. The lessons in this chapter will guide your young writers through this process step-by-step, from helping them identify what an opinion is to getting a jump start on researching their topics.

> Student and Teacher Roles

In this beginning phase of writing opinion and persuasive papers, your students need to take on the role of explorers by examining as many different topics as they can. Hopefully, they will be able to identify a number of topics that will interest them enough to engage them from start to finish.

Your instructional goals may or may not coincide with your students' interests. With a little creative thinking, you can usually overcome this obstacle and guide your students toward issues that interest them *and* meet your educational requirements. For example, if you are a social studies teacher and you want opinion papers about current events, but your students seem interested only in music and TV, ask them to examine the issues that are being explored in song lyrics or in the themes of their favorite TV shows. An idea hatched in this way often ignites great student enthusiasm.

> Expectations for an Opinion Paper

Expectations for an Opinion Paper (see page 10) sets the expectations for this entire instructional block. It is a good idea to give each student a copy of this reproducible so that you can refer to it as you focus on each required skill. Let students know that the expectations relate to the items that will be on the scoring rubric used to grade their papers. This will help them understand the importance of the expectations.

> The *Identifying Issues* Instructional Block

Because *Step One—Identifying Issues* is so critical to writing successful opinion and persuasive papers, it should be the first thing taught. The lessons in this chapter are designed to get your students thinking about possible issues, and then fine-tuning those issues down to manageable topics. In addition, students will begin to research the issues that they identify in order to discover which ones offer the best opportunities for further exploration.

The instructional block presented here is based on a five-day schedule. Depending on the needs of your students, you may wish to extend this schedule. Students will frequently need (and want) more than one day to explore topics. Others will need more time to narrow their topics down or to do research. Adjust the timing of the lessons as you see fit.

Each writing lesson has been paired with a recommended reading lesson. The five-day block in the following chart assumes that you have both a reading and a writing period in the same day. If you do not traditionally pair a reading lesson with a writing lesson, you'll need to adjust the block accordingly. To get the most out of the lessons, you should teach them in order. Note that I sometimes recommend that the reading lesson be taught before the writing lesson with which it is paired.

Day	Lesson Name	Description
Day 1: Writing	Understanding Fact vs. Opinion	Students will practice writing factual statements and statements of opinion.
Day 1: Reading	Recording Facts and Opinions	Students will read magazines and newspapers to find facts and opinions.
Day 2: Writing	Exploring Topics	Students will generate lists of topics by skimming magazines and newspapers.
Day 2: Reading	Exploring Topics In Magazines and Newspapers	Students will read some of the articles they skimmed in the writing lesson.
Day 3: Reading	Broad and Narrow Topics	Students will read their magazines and newspapers to identify both the broad and narrow topics discussed.
Day 3: Writing	Narrowing Topics	Students will begin to narrow the topics they identified on Day 2. They will write several sentences about their initial thoughts on the topics they identified.
Day 4: Writing	Researching an Opinion	Students will think about the research they will need to do for their topics.
Day 4: Reading	Conducting Research	Students will begin looking for quotes, statistics, pictures, and other information for their papers.
Day 5: Reading	Conducting Research—Day Two	Students will continue looking for quotes, statistics, graphics, pictures, and other information for their papers.
Day 5: Writing	Writing a Proposal Letter	Students will write a letter to you, summarizing their topics and their research.

On page 25, you will find optional lesson ideas for *Step One—Identifying Issues*. These lessons, while optional, will help to reinforce the difference between fact and opinion, and will immerse your students in opinion writing. These optional lessons can fit anywhere in the instructional block, but Optional Lesson Ideas A and B are a good way to introduce the concept of fact vs. opinion to students who need reinforcement in those skills.

Expectations for an Opinion Paper

After exploring potential topics for your opinion paper, choose one that you feel interested in. Research your topic to make sure you have enough material to adequately express an opinion. Follow the guidelines below.

In your opinion paper, be sure to:

- ✓ Introduce your paper with an interesting hook and a lead paragraph that states the main points you plan to make.

- ✓ Include a clear thesis statement in which you state exactly what you are for or against.

- ✓ Write paragraphs with clear topic sentences and support them with specific details and ideas.

- ✓ Organize your paper in order of importance or reverse order of importance.

- ✓ Include a strong clincher argument at the beginning or end of your paper, depending on your organization.

- ✓ Leave out unnecessary or inaccurate details.

- ✓ Conclude by restating the main thesis and making a statement of probable outcome should the reader adopt your opinion.

Remember to check your paper for correct spelling, grammar, punctuation, and usage.

Lesson 1: Understanding Fact vs. Opinion

Why Teach It?

While it's easy to assume that students know the difference between facts and opinions, the truth is that many students have a hard time distinguishing between them. Often, if an opinion seems correct, or if the student agrees with it, he considers it to be a fact. Without knowing the difference, your student writers may have difficulty in choosing an appropriate topic.

In their papers, students must support their opinions with facts; this first lesson will prepare them for that task. As a bonus, this lesson will help students on standardized tests, which often ask several questions regarding fact and opinion.

Materials Needed

- Writing notebooks (students will need these every day, for every lesson in this book).
- *Fact vs. Opinion* reproducible (see page 13).

Opening the Lesson

Explain to your students that they will be writing an opinion paper in this genre unit, and the first step is to make sure that they fully understand what an opinion is. Explain that an *opinion* is a belief or a personal view that cannot be proved. A *fact* is something that is true or is universally believed to be true. Inform them that the best way to tell fact from opinion is to ask themselves whether there is there any way they can prove a statement to be true. If there is, it's a fact. If not, it's an opinion, no matter how much they believe it to be true.

Modeling the Skill

Hand out the *Fact vs. Opinion* reproducible or show it on an overhead so that you can model the skill (see page 13). The first one has been done so that you can further explain fact and opinion. You will probably want to do the next two examples with the class to give them a little practice and check their comprehension of the concept. When you're sure they understand the task, have them complete the remaining blanks on their own. Review the answers when they are done.

Work Time

For work time, tell your students to create a "Fact vs. Opinion" page in their writer's notebook and to draw a table like the one you have modeled for them. Ask them to record at least five opinions and five facts using use whatever topics they wish in the "Topics" column.

Closing Activity

By the end of this lesson, each student will have a number of facts and opinions recorded in his or her writer's notebook. A fun and engaging way to close this activity is to rapidly call on each student to read either one of the facts or one of the opinions they've recorded, and have the class chorally respond "Fact!" or "Opinion!" Not only is this an enjoyable closing activity, but it gives you a chance to gauge your students' understanding as the lesson concludes.

Recommended Reading Lesson: Recording Facts and Opinions

As mentioned in chapter 1, you and your students should have begun gathering newspapers, magazines, and non-fiction books in preparation for this unit. Now is the time to begin using them.

A natural extension of this writing lesson is to have students read non-fiction material and record whatever facts and opinions they find. Besides reinforcing the writing lesson, this will also begin preparing them for the next lesson, in which they will start exploring possible topics for their opinion papers.

Fact vs. Opinion

PART ONE: Your job is to fill in the blanks in the table below. Write in either a fact or an opinion in the blank space for each topic. The first one has been done for you.

TOPIC	FACT	OPINION
Sports	My team has 27 wins and only 4 losses.	My team is the best team in the league!
Education		Math is my favorite subject.
Science	The sun is 93 million miles from Earth.	
History		The Civil War was the worst war in US history.
Math	2+2=4	
Music		Beethoven was a great composer.

PART TWO: Create a page in your writer's notebook called "Fact vs. Opinion." Create a table like the one above and record at least five opinions and five facts. You may use whatever topics you wish in the "Topics" column.

Lesson 2: Exploring Topics

Why Teach It?

Topic exploration may well be the most important component of teaching opinion and persuasive papers. Students need to choose a topic that truly engages them or their interest will wane long before they complete their final drafts. Giving students ownership interest in their topics keeps them engaged throughout the process.

It is not uncommon for young writers to claim that they aren't interested in *any* topics, or at least none of the topics in a given subject area. What they usually mean is that they can't immediately think of any good topics. This lesson gives them a chance to explore what they really are interested in. Because students are called on to brainstorm rather than to make a choice, it takes the pressure off and gives them a chance to reflect before committing to a topic.

As students work on generating lists of topics, you can circulate around the room, reviewing student work and pointing out which topics you think would work best. Doing this allows you to guide students into making good choices while still leaving them with the feeling that the choice was theirs.

Materials Needed

- Magazines, newspapers, and copies of tables of contents from magazines.
- The sample *Table of Contents* reproducible (see page 16). If you are teaching a content area, you may wish to use an actual table of contents from a magazine that deals with your subject area.
- Chart paper and markers.

Opening the Lesson

Begin by telling your students that topic selection may well be the most important phase of the unit. Good papers start with good topics. Ask them to look at the *Table of Contents* reproducible (see page 16). Use the first article title and tell the class you're going to list what you think the article is going to be about in your own words. On chart paper or an overhead, write "Tax Cuts." Explain that at this point, you don't need to record the whole title or any details—you are simply looking to record as many possible ideas as you can.

Modeling the Skill

Demonstrate how you can get more than one topic from the second entry on the *Table of Contents*. Add possible topics such as "Space Exploration," "Cost of Space Exploration," and "Waste in the Space Program" to your chart. At this point, you can either continue modeling the skill or you can ask the students to start listing possible topics based on the rest of the reproducible. Add them all to your chart.

Work Time

Have your students work in groups. Ask them to examine the newspapers, magazines, and tables of contents they've gathered. Have them each create a writer's notebook page called "Possible Topics" and ask them to record whatever topics they may find. At this point, have them record everything; they will have a chance to narrow their topics down in subsequent lessons. Allow them 15-20 minutes to explore. Ask each group to write down their topics on chart paper.

Closing Activity

To close the lesson, you may ask groups to present their findings to the class. As each group presents, remind the rest of the class to jot down any new topics they hear. In this way, everyone in the class will have a fairly lengthy list of topics to begin with. As a final activity, ask students to put a star next to topics they think they might have an interest in exploring further as possible topics for their opinion piece.

Recommended Reading Lesson: Exploring Topics in Magazines and Newspapers

While the focus of the writing lesson is to have students generate as many topics as they can, giving students an opportunity to actually read about the topics they have chosen will get them thinking about whether they truly want to explore those topics in their opinion papers. Ask students to find and read articles about the topics that they placed a star next to in the closing activity of the writing lesson. You may ask them to revise and refine their lists after they have had the opportunity to read about their possible topics.

Sample Table of Contents

TEEN TOPICS MAGAZINE

Lesson 3: Narrowing Topics

Why Teach It?

In the previous lesson, your students discovered many different topics and began narrowing them down by putting stars next to the ones that interested them the most. However, the scope of many of the topics they starred will be too broad for an opinion paper. For example, if they chose "Sports" as one of their choices, they now will have to look for narrow angles they can discuss in their opinion papers. "Sports" is too broad, but "The need for mandatory drug testing in baseball" is not.

This lesson is important because narrow topics help students focus their thinking. Also, the more narrow the topic, the easier it will be for your students to find support for their opinion and persuasive papers down the road. This lesson may also help your students decide whether certain topics are really right for them.

Materials Needed

- The "Possible Topics" charts students generated in their notebooks during the previous lesson.
- The *Narrowing Topics* reproducible on page 19.

Opening the Lesson

Have students examine the *Narrowing Topics* reproducible with you. Explain how the first broad topic, "World Hunger," is too vague for an opinion piece. What about world hunger? A narrower topic might be "Increasing food aid for poor countries." Discuss how this narrower topic is much more specific and focuses on a position for the opinion paper: that we either should or should not increase food aid to poor countries.

Modeling the Skill

Continue with the next broad topic on the reproducible, "Sports." Think aloud about how you could write about almost anything related to sports. Point out that there are too many choices.

Model how to narrow the topic by making suggestions and adding them to the chart. Possible narrow topics for sports might include "Should baseball use instant replays?" or "Should girls be allowed on boy's sports teams?" Make sure you impress on the class that with these narrow topics, they can take a position for an opinion paper: you may think that we should or should not use instant replays in baseballs, or you may think that we should or should not allow girls on boys' sports teams. Depending on student understanding, you may wish to model another example for them.

When you're satisfied that the students know what to do, ask them to finish the chart themselves. After a reasonable amount of time, have the class share their results.

You may wish to have your students do the Recommended Reading Lesson (below) before continuing.

Work Time

Ask your students to open their writing notebooks to the previous "Possible Topics" lesson. If your students did the closing for Lesson Two, they should have placed stars next to the topics that really interest them. If not, ask them to star the topics they are interested in now.

Ask students to create a chart in their notebooks like the *Narrowing Topics* reproducible chart you just completed. Have them start filling in the chart with the topics they put a star next to. Let them work on narrowing down any topics that are too broad. Tell them that their goal for the work period is to come up with at least five possible narrow topics.

Closing Activity

Have volunteers read from their charts, stating some of their original topics and their newly narrowed topics. Encourage the class to discuss whether the new topics are sufficiently narrow. After this discussion, have students identify three of their own narrow topics that they might want to explore further when research begins.

Recommended Reading Lesson: Broad and Narrow Topics

Using the magazines and newspapers from the previous lesson, have student skim articles to find both "broad" and "narrow" topics. Have them use a chart to track what they discover as they read. For example, a chart might look like this:

BROAD TOPIC	NARROW TOPIC
Space Exploration	NASA's budget
Movies	Violence in the movies

Narrowing Topics

BROAD TOPIC	NARROW TOPIC
World Hunger	We should increase food aid for poor countries.
Sports	
Energy Use	
Government	
Entertainment	
Guns	
Homework	
Our Neighborhood	

Lesson 4: Researching an Opinion

Why Teach It?

Before your students move into the next phase of writing an opinion paper, which is the actual crafting of the piece, you'll need to make sure that they have enough material to work with. Nothing halts progress on an opinion paper faster than when a student realizes that he or she has little to say about the topic other than a statement of belief. This lesson is designed to get your students thinking about the kinds of evidence they will need to support their opinion.

Some students may go through this lesson only to find that there really isn't enough research out there to help them support their opinions. If so, now is the time for them to find out so that they can choose another, more appropriate topic before drafting actually begins.

Materials Needed

- The *Narrowing Topics* page students completed in their notebooks in Step One, Lesson 3.
- The *Researching an Opinion* reproducible on page 22.

Opening the Lesson

Tell your students that it's time to find out which of their narrow topics they can easily support with some research. Explain that it's not enough just to offer an opinion—they must also back that opinion up with facts. To begin their research, there are four basic questions they should ask.

1. Who could I quote or interview?
2. What reference works might I use?
3. What statistics might help?
4. What pictures or illustrations can I use?

Modeling the Skill

Use a blank overhead of the *Researching an Opinion* reproducible or copy the questions on chart paper. Tell your students that you were thinking of writing on the topic of reinstating the military draft. Demonstrate how you might plan your support for that topic:

1. **Who could you quote or interview?** Politicians (quotes), my brother who is 18 (interview)

2. **What reference works might you use?** History books, encyclopedia articles on the draft, recruiting materials.

3. **What statistics might help?** Number of people currently in the military. Number of soldier needed to fight a war. An opinion poll about the draft.

4. **What pictures or illustrations can I use?** An army recruiting station. Pictures of soldiers.

Work Time

Give each student a copy of the *Researching an Opinion* reproducible (or have them copy the questions from the overhead and into their notebooks). Remind them that in Lesson 3: Narrowing Topics, they chose three topics that they wanted to begin researching. For each of those three topics, have them answer the four questions. Allow enough time for students to explore answers for all three of their potential topics.

Closing Activity

Have students share their work with their group. Allow each group member to read his or her notebook entry aloud. Then, give the group the opportunity to offer feedback. Group members may be aware of interviewees, periodicals, newspapers, pictures, or Internet resources that the individual student is unfamiliar with. This closing gives each group member a final opportunity to add to the list of resources that need to be researched before drafting takes place.

Recommended Reading Lesson: Conducting Research

This is an excellent time to bring your students to the school library for further research. Now that they know what they are looking for, allow them to explore the library to find quotes, pictures, and statistics that they can use to support their opinions. Have them bring their notebooks to the library so they can record the information they find and in what resource they found it. Make sure they research all three of their topics so they can decide which one has the most factual information to back it up.

If you have access to a computer lab or enough computers in your classroom, you may wish to let students do additional reading and research online.

It will take at least two periods for students to adequately research their topics. Give them plenty time to explore. After their research concludes, they can begin working on the culminating activity for the *Step One—Identifying Issues* section of this book, which is writing a proposal letter.

Researching an Opinion

For this exercise, you will need the three topics you worked on in **Lesson 3: Narrowing Topics**. For each of those narrow topics, answer the four research questions.

Narrow Topic 1:

    1. **Who could you quote or interview?**

    2. **What reference works might you use?**

    3. **What statistics might help?**

    4. **What pictures or illustrations can I use?**

_____

Narrow Topic 2:

    1. **Who could you quote or interview?**

    2. **What reference works might you use?**

    3. **What statistics might help?**

    4. **What pictures or illustrations can I use?**

_____

Narrow Topic 3:

    1. **Who could you quote or interview?**

    2. **What reference works might you use?**

    3. **What statistics might help?**

    4. **What pictures or illustrations can I use?**

Lesson 5: Writing a Proposal Letter

Why Teach It?

A proposal letter is a great tool for both teachers and students. By writing it, students will have an idea whether they really have enough to say about the topic. By reading it, you'll be able to approve topics that should work or reject those that won't, explaining why and making suggestions that will put students on the right path.

Materials Needed

- Writer's notebooks.
- Copies of the *Model Proposal Letter and Rubric* on page 24.

Opening the Lesson

Tell students that to write about their preferred topic, they will have to show you that they have a good handle on it by writing you a proposal letter. Let them know that there are only two criteria to make their proposals acceptable:

1. They must have an appropriate and narrow topic.
2. They must show that they can support their opinion on that topic.

Modeling the Skill

Review the *Model Proposal Letter* with the class (see page 24). Point out how the first brief paragraph clearly states the narrow topic and the position the writer will take. The second paragraph answers the four questions for research.

Work Time

Have students draft their letters to you in their notebooks.

Closing Activity

Have students share their drafts with each other and suggest changes and improvements. Students can either write their final drafts following the share time or complete them as homework. Have them attach a copy of the *Model Proposal Letter and Rubric* to their draft.

Model Proposal Letter and Rubric

10/12/07

Dear Mrs. Jones,

After giving it a lot of thought, I have decided to write about school lunches for my opinion paper. I have decided that this would make a great topic for your class because every student in this school eats school lunch 5 days a week. I plan to offer the opinion that school lunches need to be healthier.

I've done some research on this opinion, and I believe I can back it up. I plan to use quotes from the USDA and to interview our school principal and lunch aides. I plan to use reference works such as *Prevention* magazine and the encyclopedia article on nutrition. One statistic that I can use is that childhood obesity has risen 20% in the last 5 years. I also plan to use pictures of actual school lunches to help my readers understand the issue.

I hope you approve my proposal. I look forward to writing it!

Sincerely,

Sally Sandwich

Rubric for Proposal Letter

Did your Proposal Letter:	Good	Needs Work
State a narrow topic and take a position?	Topic is narrow enough and your position is clear.	Topic may need more narrowing or you may need to take a clearer position.
State your source of quotes?	Source of quotes and interviewee is clear.	Source of quotes and interviewee is unclear.
State your research sources?	States sources and those sources seem acceptable for this paper.	Does not state sources or sources may not be acceptable for this paper.
State statistics?	States at least one relevant statistic that you plan to use.	Does not state any statistics or statistic is not relevant.
State source of pictures?	Pictures cite and seem relevant to the topic.	Pictures not cited or do not seem relevant to the topic.

_____APPROVED! You're ready to start working on your opinion paper!

_____ Address the issues in the "Needs Work" column before you begin.

COMMENTS:

> Optional Lesson Ideas: Identifying Issues

Optional Lesson Idea A: Getting Immersed in Opinions

This lesson can be taught prior to the first lesson in Step One, or immediately following it. It's always a good idea to start a new writing piece by immersing your students in the genre in some way. For opinion writing, an excellent way to do this is by having your students decorate both the covers of their writing notebooks and your classroom with opinions. As a writing exercise, you can throw out a number of one word prompts, such as *school, science, books, government, America, pollution, sports, music,* and so on. Ask students to write a one sentence opinion about each topic. You can have them use markers to decorate their writing notebooks with these statements or have them create charts. They can add in illustrations as well.

As a reading exercise, have students read their magazines and cut out advertisements that make statements of opinion. You can have them cut out just the words or the pictures associated with them as well. They can decorate their notebooks or the classroom with the opinions they find.

These lessons serve the dual purpose of getting your student writers thinking about opinions while offering an opportunity to decorate your room with easily generated student work.

Optional Lesson Idea B: Writing a Fact and Opinion Autobiography

Two things most students love to do are writing about themselves and drawing. This lesson lets them do both. Ask your students to divide a sheet of construction paper or chart paper in half lengthwise, and to reserve a box in the center for a drawing. They should title the page "My Fact and Opinion Autobiography." On the left side of they paper they should write facts about themselves, and on the right side, they should write opinions about themselves. After they are done writing, ask them to draw a picture of themselves that reflects the facts and opinions they have written down. For example, if one of their opinions is "I am smart" they might draw themselves with a graduation cap or holding a report card covered with A's. Ask students to present their autobiographies as a closing to the lesson.

This lesson reinforces the distinction between fact and opinion. You may also use this lesson to create decorations for your classroom that immerse your students in the opinion-writing genre.

Optional Lesson Idea C: Measure for Measure

One way to help students distinguish fact from fiction is to show them that many facts can be measured in some way. Ask students to free-write about some topic that is familiar to them, such as their school or their classroom. Instruct them to use as much description as possible. When they are done, ask them to make two lists: one with all the facts in their descriptions and one with all the opinions. Ask them to write down how they might measure the facts about their topics. Let them know that if they can't measure their "fact" in some way, it might well be an opinion.

Show them an example like this to get them started:

Measure for Measure

FACT	OPINION
This classroom is blue. I can measure that with a color chart.	This classroom is colorful.
This room is a 20' x 15' rectangle. I can measure that with a ruler or tape measure.	This room is big.

Point out to students that no matter how colorful or big they think the room is, the words *big* and *colorful* are subjective, relative, and non-specific, and therefore they are a matter of opinion.

This lesson will get your students thinking about the language used to distinguish between fact and opinion.

Optional Lesson Idea D: Skinny Topics

Narrowing topics down often presents a great challenge for students. Sometimes they truly don't understand how to narrow their topics, but often they fear that narrow topics won't offer them enough to write about. This simple exercise shows students that narrowing topics is easy, and helps allay their fears by helping them create a number of topics that are more than sufficient for an opinion paper.

I often tell students that we're going to put their topics on a diet: to make them skinny! Give your class a number of broad topics, and let them use an organizer like the one below to think through how they might drop some weight from those topics. Use the sample below to show them how to do it.

Skinny Topics

Fat Topic
Science

Skinnier Topic
Pollution

Skinnier Topic
Animals

Skinny Topic
Nuclear energy

Skinny Topic
Car exhaust

Skinny Topic
Animal testing

Skinny Topic
Endangered species

You can continue on with these topics by asking your students to keep branching off until they find the narrowest topics they can.

CHAPTER 3
Step Two—Crafting an Opinion Paper

Organization is the key to a successful opinion paper.

While that may seem self-evident, students must be taught the various Target Skills that will allow them to successfully organize, and then craft, their opinion papers. They must learn not only how to begin and end their papers, but also what goes in between. They must make decisions about how to structure their information, including the order of their paragraphs as well as the order of the information within each paragraph.

This chapter will help you teach your students all of these skills. In addition to helping your students craft an excellent opinion paper, these skills can also help them understand the concepts behind writing the classic "five-paragraph essay" that is now commonly found on standardized writing tests at virtually every grade level.

Many of the lessons here include the use of a graphic organizer to assist your students in getting their ideas in order. This makes composing easier, and helps your students realize that good writers make decisions about their writing throughout the entire process.

> Scoring Rubric for an Opinion Paper

At the end of this chapter (see page 47) there is a rubric that you may use as-is or adapt for your own needs. The rubric sets out exactly what your students will need to include in their opinion papers. It should be given out following Lesson 6 so that students know exactly how they will be graded before they begin writing the final copies of their drafts. The rubric is also helpful as a tool for peer editing, as students can evaluate each other using the same criteria you will use when you grade the papers.

Also available at the end of the chapter is a sample paper that you may share with your students (see page 48). Discuss it in terms of the rubric. It should rate a 3 or 4 in most criteria.

> The *Crafting an Opinion Paper* Instructional Block

The purpose of this instructional block is to get your young writers thinking about how they will craft their opinion pieces. They will be asked to think about thesis statements, hooks and leads, closings, and organization (of each paragraph, and of the paper as a whole).

The instructional block presented here is based on a seven-day schedule. Depending on the needs of your students, you may wish to extend some of the lessons over a longer period of time. You may need an additional day or two for actual drafting and peer editing.

Each writing lesson has been paired with a recommended reading lesson. The seven-day block in the following chart assumes that you have both a reading and a writing period in the same day. If you do not traditionally pair a reading lesson with a writing lesson, you'll need to adjust the block accordingly. To get the most out of the lessons, you should teach them in order. Note that I sometimes recommend that the reading lesson be taught before the writing lesson with which it is paired.

Day	Lesson Name	Description
Day 1: Reading	Identifying Thesis Statements	Students will read Op-Ed pieces and magazine articles to find the thesis statement.
Day 1: Writing	Writing a Thesis Statement	Students will write a *for* or *against* statement that will form the thesis of their opinion paper.
Day 2: Reading	Identifying Support	Students will read to find the facts, quotes, and pictures used to support a thesis in an article.
Day 2: Writing	Supporting Your Thesis	Students will create a graphic organizer of facts, quotes, and pictures that support the thesis of their opinion paper.
Day 3: Writing	Organizing Your Information/ Finding a Clincher	Students will place their organizers from the previous day in both order of importance and reverse order of importance, and then identify their clincher argument.
Day 3: Reading	Deciding Order of Importance	Students will read articles to determine whether the article is written with the information in order of importance or reverse order of importance.
Day 4: Writing	Writing the Hook and Lead Paragraph	Students will identify a hook from the facts in their research, and write their opening paragraphs.
Day 4: Reading	Examining Hooks	Students will browse magazine and newspaper articles looking for and recording interesting hooks.
Day 5: Reading	Examining Main Ideas and Support—Day One	Students will read to find topic sentences and the support used. Includes an examination of topic sentence placement and amount of support needed.
Day 5: Writing	Writing the Body—Day One	Students will complete graphic organizers showing their topic sentences and support. They work on proper organization of information.
Day 6: Reading	Examining Main Ideas and Support—Day Two	Students will engage in additional practice of the day 5 reading skill.
Day 6: Writing	Writing the Body—Day Two	Students will write their body paragraphs from their organizers, experimenting with topic sentence placement.
Day 7: Reading	Examining Closings	Students will browse magazine and newspaper articles looking for and recording interesting closings.
Day 7: Writing	Closing Type: Probable Outcomes	Student will write a concluding paragraph that restates the thesis and the probable result of adopting the opinion.

On page 45, you will find optional lesson ideas for this step. These lessons, while optional, will assist your students in adding professional touches to their opinion papers, such as adding sidebars, pictures with captions, and graphs. There are lessons to teach optimal use of quotes as well as using transitions.

Lesson 1: Writing a Thesis Statement

Why Teach It?

Teaching your students to turn their opinion into a thesis statement is important to the development of both their reading and writing skills.

The ability to quickly identify the thesis of a piece of writing is a key to understanding that piece. For this reason, standardized tests frequently ask students to identify the main idea—that is, the thesis—of a piece of writing. As writers, students need to state the thesis of their papers succinctly. This gets them focused on exactly what they want to say and how they will support their idea.

Materials Needed

- The *Narrowing Topics* charts created in Step One, Lesson 3.
- Student proposal letters.

Opening the Lesson

Begin by defining a *thesis* as *the subject being considered in an essay*. Explain further that the thesis is the statement that they hope to support in their opinion papers.

Modeling the Skill

Ask students to return to their *Narrowing Topics* charts in their notebooks. Ask volunteers to list some of their topics for the class. Take a few of those topics and turn them into thesis statements. A good way to model this is by showing that most opinion topics have a *for* and *against* side to them, and that their thesis statement can reflect a pro or con stance. For example, if a student offers a narrow topic of "Pollution in our city," show them that it can have both a for and against side: "I am FOR spending more tax money to clean up this city" or "I am AGAINST spending more tax money to clean up this city." Point out that both these statements are opinions that must be supported.

You may wish to begin this lesson with the Recommended Reading Lesson below.

Work Time

You may wish to have students practice creating thesis statements from some of their narrow topics. When you are satisfied that they understand this process, ask them to review their proposal letters. Have them write a FOR or AGAINST statement that will form the thesis of their opinion piece.

Closing Activity

Have students share their thesis statements with the rest of the class. Have the class evaluate whether there is an adequate FOR or AGAINST statement contained in the thesis.

Recommended Reading Lesson: Identifying Thesis Statements

Model this skill yourself by reading an opinion piece with your students. Identify the thesis and highlight sentences that pointed you to that thesis. Then, allow your students to read the opinion pieces you gathered and have them write down what they believe is the thesis of each article they read. You may also want to ask them to identify the clues that led them to the thesis.

Lesson 2: Supporting Your Thesis

Why Teach It?

The ability to support a thesis statement is the foundation for almost all the non-fiction writing your students will do in their academic careers. Teaching them how to support their ideas will help your students write across the curriculum, and it will improve their performance on written standardized tests.

Many students believe that opinions are just opinions, and since none of them can be proved, they are all of equal value. This lesson will help them begin to understand that while opinions do not have the same truth value as facts, there are nevertheless strong opinions and weak opinions.

Materials Needed

- Student thesis statements.
- Copies of the *Supporting a Thesis* graphic organizer on page 32.

Opening the Lesson

Discuss the idea of weak opinions vs. strong opinions with your class. Emphasize that strong opinions are ones backed by factual information, expert quotes, anecdotal information, and statistics. Pictures and other graphics help reinforce opinions by giving the reader a chance to see for him or herself exactly what the writer is discussing

Modeling the Skill

Give each student a copy of the *Supporting a Thesis* graphic organizer. Review the three main types of support you asked your students to find during their research: Facts (statistics), quotes/interviews, and pictures.

Give them a model opinion thesis, such as "This classroom should be more colorful." Review some facts with them about the room (How many colors are there? Color charts? Color pictures?). Ask for any other facts they can supply to support the thesis. Record student responses as you progress.

Move on to quotes/interviews, and make up a quote you might use (Principal Levin said, "This room looks like a black-and-white TV show from the 50's!"). Ask who else might offer a valid opinion on this thesis (parents, other teachers, etc.). Finally, point out a section of the room that could use more color. Tell students that a photo of this part of the room could help prove your thesis. Ask for more possible places in this room that might make good photographic evidence. Chart all the information you've gathered. Ask students to evaluate whether the evidence makes for a strong opinion that is supported by facts and information, or a weak opinion that is mostly unsupported.

In order to show your students how professional writers support their theses, you should teach the Recommended Reading Lesson (below) before continuing.

Work Time

Ask students to fill in their own graphic organizers with the research they gathered in Step One, Lesson 4 on page 20. Have them start by filling in the Thesis Statement at the top of the organizer, and then the facts, quotes, and photos they may use as support in their opinion papers.

Closing Activity

Ask groups to share their organizers. Each member should have an opportunity to read his or her organizer to their group and explain how the evidence helps support the thesis and create a strong opinion. Have each group choose one student organizer that they feel presents the strongest evidence to support the thesis. Ask chosen students to present to the rest of the class. You may wish to have the class vote on whether they think each opinion is weak or strong, based upon the evidence provided in the organizer.

Recommended Reading Lesson: Identifying Support

Ask students to fill in a *Supporting a Thesis* sheet for an opinion article they are reading. They should record the thesis of the article, the facts and statistics used by the authors, any quotes or interviews the article contains, and the pictures or illustrations used.

To close the lesson, you may ask students to summarize the article they read using only their organizers. Have them offer an opinion as to whether the article they read offered strong support of the thesis and what additional information might have made the article stronger.

Supporting a Thesis

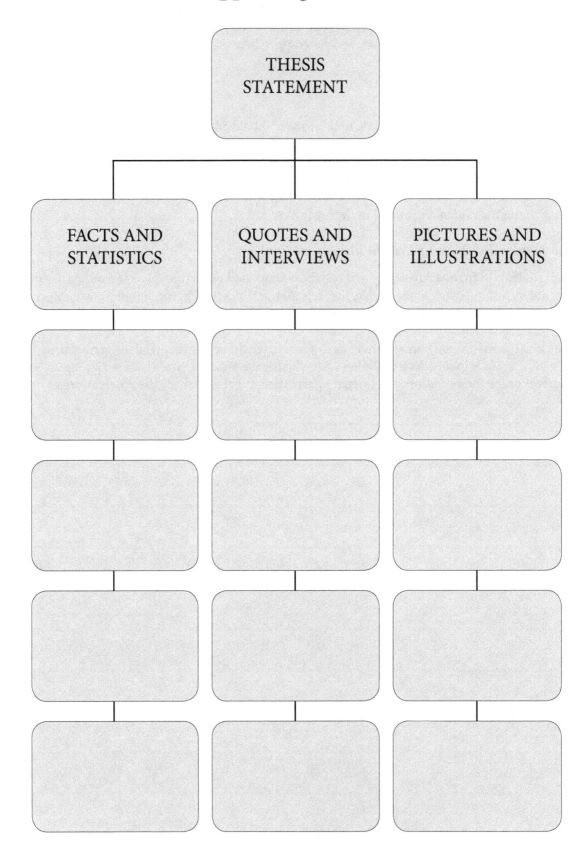

THESIS
STATEMENT

FACTS AND
STATISTICS

QUOTES AND
INTERVIEWS

PICTURES AND
ILLUSTRATIONS

Lesson 3: Organizing Your Information/Finding a Clincher

Why Teach It?

Organization is key to any essay. By now, your students have generated a lot of ideas and done a considerable amount of research on their topics. Explain to them that unless this information is organized and presented in a logical fashion, the opinion piece will seem little more than a haphazard collection of information.

This lesson teaches two types of organization: *order of importance* and *reverse order of importance*. These types of organization work particularly well with opinion pieces, and can generate discussion among your students as to which works best, leading to some very deep thinking about both structure of the writing piece and the quality of the information used to present the opinion.

This lesson also teaches your students to identify their *clincher*, or their best supporting detail.

Materials Needed

- Student organizers from the previous lesson.
- The *Organizing Your Information* graphic organizer on page 35.

Opening the Lesson

Explain to students that the organization of their piece is extremely important, and you want them to spend some time thinking about the best arrangement of their information. Tell them you'll be looking at two forms of organization: *order of importance* and *reverse order of importance*. For *order of importance*, the supporting details are presented from least important to most important, and for *reverse order of importance* the order of details is reversed, from most important to least important.

Define the word *clincher* for your class as *the supporting detail that best supports the opinion*. Tell them that when using an order of importance organization, the clincher comes last, and that for reverse order of importance the clincher comes first.

Modeling the Skill

Ask students to imagine that they are writing an opinion paper about the need to improve school lunches. Either on a chart or an overhead, write the following information:

> **Thesis:** We need healthier school lunches that kids will eat.
> **Supporting Detail 1:** Kids like food that tastes good and is good for them.
> **Supporting Detail 2:** Eating nutritious food helps students perform better academically.
> **Supporting Detail 3**: Many students don't eat nutritious meals outside of school.
> **Supporting Detail 4:** Nutritious food helps cut down on childhood obesity.

Model your thinking about which details are the most convincing. While detail 1 is true, it is also true that kids like lunches that are bad for them, so this is probably the weakest detail. While the remaining details all seem important, detail 2 is probably the most important to students and the schools, and therefore this is the *clincher*.

Then show the students the following (or use an overhead of *Organizing Your Information* and actually fill in the details):

ORDER OF IMPORTANCE: Detail 1, ___, ___, 2.
REVERSE ORDER OF IMPORTANCE: Detail 2, ___, ___, 1.

Have students help you fill in the blanks with what they think is the correct order and reverse order for the details. Ask them to explain their reasoning.

Work Time

Ask students to take out their *Supporting a Thesis* organizers from the previous writing lesson. Tell them to evaluate their details, and number them 1-4 (or however many details they have) in order of importance, with the last detail being the most important, or the clincher. Then ask them to write the details on the graphic organizer called *Organizing Your Information*.

Closing Activity

Ask your students to reflect on the activity they did during work time. Have them write a paragraph in their notebooks explaining whether they think order of importance or reverse order of importance will work best for their paper. Ask them to explain their thinking in the paragraph.

Recommended Reading Lesson: Deciding Order of Importance

Ask students to read opinion pieces from their magazines or from Op-Ed pieces from newspapers. When they have finished reading, have them record the main supporting details of the opinion piece. Ask them to decide whether they think the article was written in order of importance and reverse order of importance. Also ask them what they think the author's clincher was, and whether it appeared at the beginning or the end of the article.

Organizing Your Information

Use the organizer below to put your supporting details in ORDER OF IMPORTANCE, from least important to most important. The final detail should be your clincher detail, which is the supporting detail that best supports your argument. If you choose to write your paper in reverse order of importance, simply start your writing with the detail at the bottom of the page and work backwards.

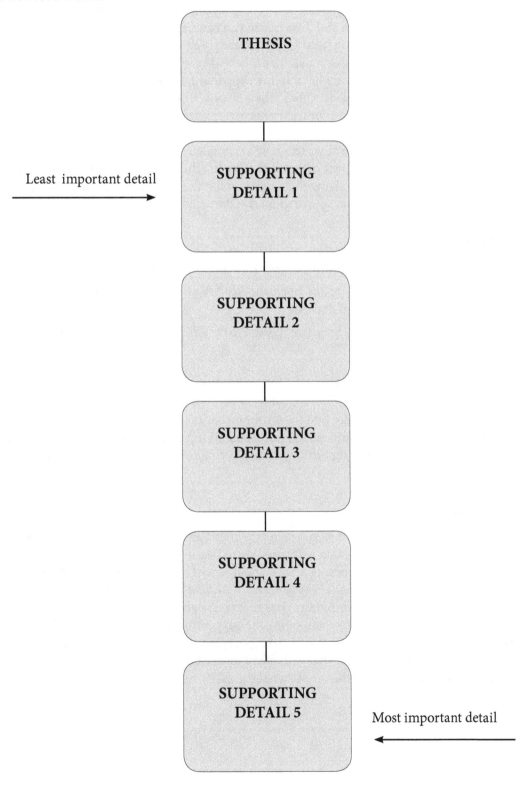

Least important detail →

THESIS

SUPPORTING DETAIL 1

SUPPORTING DETAIL 2

SUPPORTING DETAIL 3

SUPPORTING DETAIL 4

SUPPORTING DETAIL 5

← Most important detail

Lesson 4: Writing the Hook and Lead Paragraph

Why Teach It?

A good hook and lead paragraph sets the tone for the entire paper and gives the reader a reason to read on. It can also help your student writers focus in on exactly what they want to say before they begin to write the body of their opinion papers.

This lesson focuses on only one type of hook—using an interesting fact or statistic. There are, of course, many more lead types, and if you wish, you can supplement this lesson with the lead types for persuasive essays on page 74. (If you are going to have your students to develop this opinion piece into a persuasive paper, it's probably best to teach only this one lead type for now, and let students explore others later. In my experience, if you teach a variety of lead types early in the writing process, students choose their favorite and are loath to change it when the persuasive writing begins, even if another type is better suited to their topic.)

This lesson also shows your student writers how to complete their first paragraph by listing their supporting details within their opening paragraph. This is beneficial for two reasons: it keeps your writers focused by giving them a paragraph they can refer back to, and it is an excellent method for writing essay openings on standardized tests.

Materials Needed

- The research done in Step One, Lesson 4: Researching an Opinion.
- An overhead of the *Writing the Hook and Lead Paragraph* reproducible on page 38, and copies for each student, if desired.
- Student organizers from Step Two, Lesson 3: Organizing Your Information.

Opening the Lesson

Explain to your students that a *hook* is a great term because it describes exactly what it is intended to do—to grab the reader into the writing piece as if with a hook! To hook the reader effectively, a writer must begin immediately with something that will interest the reader. From there, they can enumerate their supporting details, giving the reader an idea or preview of what is to come.

Modeling the Skill

Write an opening paragraph for the class using the thesis and supporting details from the previous lesson. Inform the class that you are going to begin your opening paragraph with a hook. Model this for them by choosing a hook about school lunches. Show them the overhead, which contains the following "fact": *Fifty per cent of the food that gets served in the lunch room ends up in the garbage untouched.* Tell the class that you're going to use this statistic as your hook, and then follow the hook by mentioning the supporting details that you're going to discuss in your opinion piece. As you write your paragraph on the overhead, discuss that you're using the details in the same order that you intend to write about them in the opinion paper itself. Your last sentence will be the thesis statement itself.

The completed model paragraph will look something like this:

> *Fifty per cent of the food that gets served in the lunchroom ends up in the garbage untouched. The truth is, kids like eating food that tastes good and is good for them. However, many students don't eat nutritious meals outside of school. It's well known that nutritious food helps cut down on childhood obesity and helps students perform better academically. In my opinion, we need healthier school lunches that kids will eat.*

In order to familiarize your students with various types of hooks, you may wish to begin with the Recommended Reading Lesson that follows the writing portion of this lesson.

Work Time

Tell students that the first thing they need to do is review their research to find an interesting fact that they can use as a hook. Once they have found it, they should write their opening sentence using the hook, and follow that with their supporting details in the order they plan to write about them in bulleted form. Ask them to write a closing sentence that states their thesis just as you did in your model paragraph.

Closing Activity

A great way to close this lesson is to have your group members share their writing. Ask them to focus on whether each member has included all three parts in their opening paragraphs: a hook, the supporting details, and a statement of the thesis.

Recommended Reading Lesson: Examining Hooks

Ask your students to look for articles that begin with an interesting fact. They should record their findings in their notebooks. Ask students to write down what it was they found interesting about each hook they recorded.

Writing the Hook and Lead Paragraph

Hook: Fifty per cent of the food that comes into the lunchroom ends up in the garbage untouched.

Supporting Detail 1: Kids like food that tastes good and is good for them.

Supporting Detail 2: Many students don't eat nutritious meals outside of school.

Supporting Detail 3: Nutritious food helps cut down on childhood obesity.

Supporting Detail 4: Eating nutritious food helps students perform academically.

Thesis: We need healthier school lunches that kids will eat.

Fifty per cent of the food that comes into the lunchroom ends up in

the garbage untouched. _____

_____

_____

_____

_____

_____

_____

_____

_____

_____

Lesson 5: Writing the Body

Why Teach It?

After all the research and organization you and your students have worked on, it may seem as though the body of the paper should write itself. In most cases, it does not. Most students need to be explicitly taught, or at least explicitly reminded, of how to put together the paragraphs that will make up the body of the opinion paper.

Even if you feel your students already know how to write effective paragraphs, it will be worthwhile to teach this lesson because it follows the "topic sentence and supporting sentences" structure required now on most standardized writing tests. It also uses an organizer as a pre-writing tool, and these are found more and more frequently on standardized writing tests as well. They are often graded along with the essay.

This writing lesson often works best when it is divided over two days. On the first day, have students create their organizers, and on the next day, ask them to draft their paragraphs.

Materials Needed

- The notebook entry called *Writing the Hook* from Step Two, Lesson 4.
- The completed Model Paragraph from Step Two, Lesson 4.
- The *Writing the Body* organizer on page 42.

Opening the Lesson

Let students know that today they'll be working on organizing and drafting the body paragraphs of their opinion papers. Remind students that in the previous lesson, they crafted an opening paragraph that contained a hook, a list of topics to be discussed in the paper, and a thesis. Ask them to review those paragraphs from their notebooks and to make sure their paragraphs contain all three elements.

Modeling the Skill

Show students your opening paragraph model from the previous lesson. Discuss how the paragraph stated that you would write about four things in your opinion paper:

- Kids like food that tastes good and is good for them.
- Many students don't eat nutritious meals outside of school.
- Nutritious food helps cut down on childhood obesity.
- Eating nutritious food helps students perform academically.

Explain that each of these topics will now become a *topic sentence* for a paragraph in your opinion paper, and that you will support each one with information, statistics, and quotes that you gathered when you did your original research.

Use a transparency of the *Writing the Body* organizer and fill in each of the topic sentence boxes with one of the bulleted items. Then focus on the first one: Kids like food that tastes good and is good for them. Think aloud as you fill in the details boxes of your organizer. Try to use at least one quote and one statistic. Your completed organizer might look something like this:

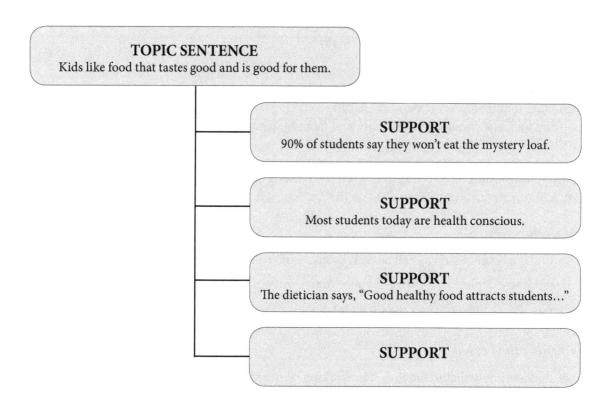

TOPIC SENTENCE
Kids like food that tastes good and is good for them.

SUPPORT
90% of students say they won't eat the mystery loaf.

SUPPORT
Most students today are health conscious.

SUPPORT
The dietician says, "Good healthy food attracts students…"

SUPPORT

Let students know that they don't have to fill in every blank in the organizer, but they should have at least two types of support for every topic sentence.

To give students a chance to see how professional writers use topic and supporting sentences, you should have them do this lesson's Recommended Reading Lesson before continuing.

Work Time, Day One

Have students complete their organizers. They should refer to their *Writing the Hook* entries for the topic sentences, and to their research for the support.

Closing Activity, Day One

Ask students to share their organizers with their writing group. As each student shares, the rest of the group should be checking to make sure that there are at least two supporting items for each topic sentence and that there is a mix of quotes and statistics throughout.

Work Time, Day Two

Begin day two by modeling how to write paragraphs using topic sentences and support. Use the organizer you modeled and think aloud as you write. Your completed paragraph may look something like this:

Kids like food that tastes good and is good for them. Most students today are health conscious and don't want to eat a lot of junk. For example, 90% of students I asked said they would not eat the mystery loaf that's usually served on Wednesdays. Our school dietician, Ms. Brody, told me that, "Good healthy food attracts students. Bad food attracts bugs."

It's also a good idea at this stage to show students that their topics sentences don't necessarily have to be the first sentence in the paragraph. Show them your paragraph with the topic sentence placed at the end, like below:

Most students today are health conscious and don't want to eat a lot of junk. For example, 90% of students I asked said they would not eat the mystery loaf that's usually served on Wednesdays. Our school dietician, Ms. Brody, told me that, "Good healthy food attracts students. Bad food attracts bugs." Simply put, kids like food that tastes good and is good for them.

Ask students to read both paragraphs and decide which one they like better and discuss why.

For student work time, have them actually begin drafting their paragraphs. Tell them that they should experiment with the placement of their topic sentences, as well as with the order of their supporting sentences. As a closing, you may wish to ask your students to read some paragraphs aloud and explain how they chose the placement and order of their sentences.

Recommended Reading Lesson: Identifying Main Ideas and Support

This is a great time to involve your students in finding topic sentences in the articles they have been reading. As they read, ask them to use a highlighter to mark the topic sentences of each paragraph in their articles. When they finish reading, ask them to write a notebook entry about what they have read. Did the author mostly place topic sentences at the beginning, end, or somewhere in the middle of paragraphs? On average, how many items of support did the author include for each topic sentence?

You can easily use this reading lesson on consecutive days as part of a double block to accompany the writing lessons. Identifying the topic sentence or main idea not only helps reading comprehension, but it is a skill that is frequently called upon on standardized tests.

If you wish, you can also ask the class to fill out the graphic organizer on the next page for the article they are reading.

Writing the Body

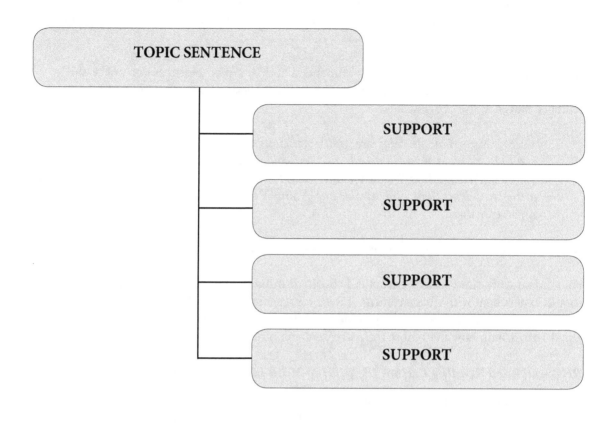

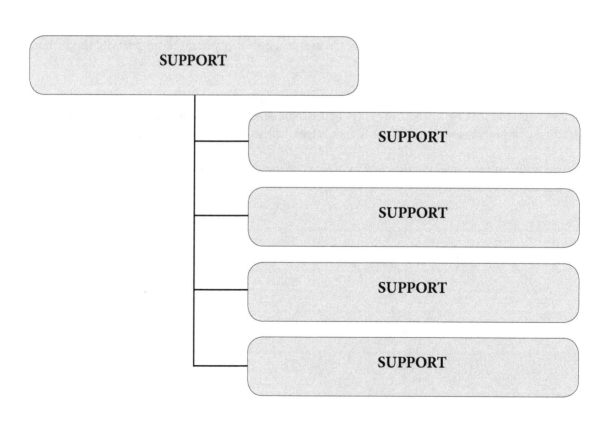

Lesson 6: Closing Type: Probable Outcomes

Why Teach It?

If you've taught writing for any length of time, you've probably seen papers that closed something like this: "Well, that's all I have to say about that! Bye!" Unless you explicitly instruct students in how to end their opinion pieces, you can expect more of the same. Student writers frequently run out of steam as they reach the closing. Having said everything they wanted to say in the body, they often find themselves at a loss as to how to close.

While it's fine for students to summarize their main points in the closing, it also lacks originality. A better way to close is to ask them to imagine the probable outcomes should their opinions be followed. There are, of course, many other closing types, and if you wish, you can supplement this lesson with the closing types for persuasive essays on page 96. In fact, if you don't intend to develop this opinion piece into a persuasive paper, you should probably give your students wider scope in choosing their closings. If, however, you do want this opinion piece to develop into a persuasive paper, it's probably best to teach this one closing type for now, and let students explore the others later.

Materials Needed

- Student drafts of the opening and body paragraphs.
- Transparency or chart of your sample thesis and topics.

Opening the Lesson

Let students know that today they'll be working on the closing for their opinion pieces. By now, the lead and body paragraphs should have been drafted. Remind students that a good closing sums up the opinion piece, gives it a sense of closure, and leaves the reader with something to think about.

Modeling the Skill

Remind students of your model thesis and topics on an overhead or chart:

THESIS: *The cafeteria should serve healthier, better tasting food.*

PARAGRAPH TOPICS:

Kids like food that tastes good and is good for them.
Many students don't eat nutritious meals outside of school.
Nutritious food helps cut down on childhood obesity.
Eating nutritious food helps students perform academically.

Tell students that you are going to briefly restate your thesis as part of your closing, and that you are going to try to think of a possible outcome should your opinion be accepted. Write a paragraph like this for students as a model:

In conclusion, it is my opinion that the cafeteria should offer healthier and better tasting food. If they do, this school can look forward to a happier, healthier, and smarter student population.

Show them that this type of paragraph always has a flip side, where you look at the possible outcome should the opinion be rejected.

> *In conclusion, it is my opinion that the cafeteria should offer healthier and better tasting food. If they don't, this school can expect to see lower academic performance and much bigger waistlines.*

Ask students to discuss with you which of these possible ending they prefer and why. Also ask them to identify where the paragraphs summarize, how they offer a sense of closure, and what each one leads the reader to think about. Remind students that writers make such decisions all the time, and they will be making such a decision as they work on concluding paragraphs during work time.

To give students a chance to see how professional writers close their opinion pieces, you should have students do the Recommended Reading Lesson (below) before continuing.

Work Time

Have students review their theses and body paragraph drafts to come up with closings that summarize and state possible outcomes. Ask them to write their closings two ways: one discussing what the outcome may be if their opinion is followed, and one discussing what the outcome will be if it is not followed. Ask them to consider both carefully and to place a star next to the one they prefer.

Closing Activity

Students should share their closings in their writing groups. Ask them to read both closings to the group without revealing which one they placed a star next to. Have the group vote on the preferred ending to see if it matches the opinion of the author.

Recommended Reading Lesson: Examining Closings

Ask your students to thumb through a number of magazines and newspaper articles looking for closings. If they find any particularly interesting ones, they can write those down in their notebooks. Also ask students to write down what it was they found interesting about the each closing they recorded.

> Optional Lesson Ideas: Crafting an Opinion Paper

Optional Lesson Idea A: Creating Sidebars

Students enjoy creating sidebars because it gives their opinion paper the feel of a magazine article. It also gives a chance to be creative with colors, layout, and possibly charts or graphs. Define *sidebars* for students: distinct pieces of text or other information that help clarify or enlarge upon the subject of an article.

Begin with a reading lesson, showing students a sidebar from an actual magazine article and exploring how it helps to highlight the information in the main body of text. Then ask students to read their magazines to find examples of sidebars. When they find them, ask them to explain how the sidebar helped clarify the text of the article.

For the writing lesson, have students review their information for something that might make an interesting sidebar. Reinforce the idea that what is in the sidebar should help highlight the information in the main body of their text.

Optional Lesson Idea B: Pairing Pictures and Captions

In the course of their research, your students likely came across many pictures and illustrations that would help get their opinions across to their audience. While a picture is useful, it is much more informative with an appropriate caption. Have your students browse their magazines for pictures with captions. Ask them to observe or record the relationship between the pictures and their captions. Do the captions inform, explain, entertain, or question? Have students share the strategies they discover. Then ask students to choose pictures for their opinion pieces, and to write captions for those pictures that either inform, explain, entertain, or question.

Optional Lesson Idea C: Titles

While it may seem a small matter, asking students to come up with a good title can engage them in some deep thinking about their topics. Challenge them to brainstorm a title that conveys the most important aspect of their opinion piece. You can kick off this lesson by asking students to browse their magazines and newspapers, and to record the titles that interest them. Ask them what technique the author used in choosing a title. Was it descriptive, a play on words, a statement of fact, or some other method? Go further by asking them to evaluate how well the title reflected the content of the article.

To continue this lesson, you can take your class to the library to hunt for title types. You can teach these types first and then ask students to find and classify titles they find:

> **Single Words:** *Jaws; Dominic; Victory*
>
> **Reversal Titles:** *One Bad Deed Deserves Another*
>
> **Rhyming Titles:** *Blocks of Rocks; Commotion in the Ocean*
>
> **Alliterative Titles:** *Boo to a Goose; Twilight Comes Twice*
>
> **Contrast Titles:** *Cold Feelings over Heated Debates*
>
> **Repetition Titles:** *Rich Dad, Poor Dad*
>
> **Parodoxical Titles:** *True Lies*
>
> **Blunt Statements:** *Sudoku for Dummies*

When it is time for students to write their own titles, have them check their ideas against the following criteria:

1. Can I pronounce it easily?
2. Is it bland?
3. Does it fit the subject matter?
4. Is it a corny cliché?
5. Is it too sweet?
6. Does it tell too much?
7. Is it memorable?

Optional Lesson Idea D: Using Transitional Words and Phrases

Explain to the class that transitional words and phrases will help their readers understand their writing better by showing them the relationships between ideas. While there are many types of transitions, this lesson will focus on the four most likely to be used in an opinion paper: *Time, Addition, Compare/Contrast,* and *Summary.* Have your student writers review the lists below, and then work on putting some transitions into their drafts.

- **TIME: Used to show order or a change in actual time.** *First, second, third, before, prior, prior to, after, afterwards, after that, at first, last, lastly, finally, after, afterwards, previously, subsequently, eventually, immediately, simultaneously.*

- **ADDITION: Used to show that something is connected to something else.** *And, in addition, additionally, in addition to, also, likewise, similarly, further, furthermore, including, together with, moreover, again, combined with.*

- **COMPARE/CONTRAST: Used to show how something is the same or different.**

    Comparison words: *In comparison, likewise, similarly, correspondingly, comparably, comparatively, in the same vein, much like.*

    Contrast words: *But, however, yet, on the other hand, in contrast, instead of, in spite of, nevertheless, conversely, versus, regardless, in distinction, in opposition.*

- **SUMMARY: Used to summarize points made.** *In summary, in conclusion, in short, in brief, finally, consequently, in consequence, as a result, accordingly, therefore, so, then, thus, as a result, hence.*

Rubric for an Opinion Paper

IN YOUR OPINION PAPER, DID YOU:	OUTSTANDING 4	GOOD 3	NEEDS IMPROVEMENT 2	NOT DONE 1
Begin with an interesting hook and a lead paragraph that clearly states what you intend to write about?	Great hook that generates reader interest and a lead paragraph that draws the reader into the opinion paper.	Good hook that interests the reader and a lead paragraph that tells the reader what the opinion paper is about.	Hook is present but doesn't truly interest the reader and the lead paragraph is unclear about what is to follow.	No hook is used, or the lead paragraph is confusing.
Include a clear thesis statement?	Thesis statement is interesting and states the position you intend to take.	Thesis statement is present and states the position you intend to take.	Thesis statement is unclear or does not clearly state the position you intend to take.	Thesis statement is not present.
Organize your topics and have a clear "clincher" argument?	Logically organized paragraphs with a well defined and convincing clincher.	Well organized paragraphs with an easily identified clincher.	Organization needs work or your clincher is not easily identified.	Little organization or clincher not present or identifiable.
Write topic sentences and adequately support them?	Interesting topic sentences with varied placement. Topic sentences are fully supported.	Good topic sentences with some variety in placement. Topic sentences are supported.	Topic sentences or placement need work. Topic sentences may not be adequately supported.	Topic sentences not clear or not present. Little if any support for topics.
Conclude by restating the thesis and make a statement of probable outcomes?	Restates the thesis and makes a statement of probable outcome that makes an impact on the reader.	Restates the thesis and makes a statement of probable outcome that is of interest to the reader.	Restatement of thesis or statement of probable outcome need work or do not interest the reader.	Restatement of thesis and statement of probable outcome either missing or confusing.
Avoid errors in grammar, spelling, punctuation, and usage?	Paper is free of errors.	Only a few minor errors that do not interfere with reader understanding.	More than a few errors. Some errors may interfere with reader understanding.	Many errors that make the paper difficult to understand.

COMMENTS:

Bad Food, Bad Performance

Fifty per cent of the food that gets served in the lunchroom ends up in the garbage untouched. The truth is, kids like eating food that tastes good and is good for them. However, many students don't eat nutritious meals outside of school. It's well known that nutritious food helps cut down on childhood obesity and helps students perform better academically. In my opinion, we need healthier school lunches that kids will eat.

Kids like food that tastes good and is good for them. Most students today are health conscious and don't want to eat a lot of junk. For example, 90% of students I asked said they would not eat the mystery loaf that's usually served on Wednesdays. Our school dietician, Ms. Brody, told me that, "Good healthy food attracts students. Bad food attracts bugs."

Many students don't eat nutritious meals outside of school. Because so many parents work outside of the home, most students are unsupervised after school, and they often eat salty snacks or sugary treats as soon as they get home. Busy parents often don't have time to cook nutritious meals and often pick up fat-laden fast food on their way home from their jobs. You can see the results of this trend by counting the growing number of obese children.

It's been proven that students who eat a healthy breakfast before taking a test do better than students who don't. Additionally, I was surprised when Mrs. Rhinehart, our debate coach, told me that she is just as strict about the debate team's diet as Coach Bronson is about the football team's. "I can tell when my team has been eating poorly," she said. "Their minds are sluggish, and they are more likely to lose a match."

In conclusion, it is my opinion that the cafeteria should offer healthier and better tasting food. If they do, this school can look forward to a happier, healthier, and smarter student population.

CHAPTER 4
Step Three—Examining Persuasive Elements

This chapter looks at the elements students will need to explore before beginning to craft persuasive essays. Among the elements critical to persuasive writing are *author's purpose, audience, criteria for evidence,* and *evaluating both sides of the topic issue.* The lessons in this chapter provide information and strategies your students need to learn so they can understand these elements and include them in a written piece.

> Starting with Persuasive Writing

Some teachers may have skipped opinion writing all together and are beginning their units with persuasive writing. Before jumping into the lessons in this chapter, you should teach some of the foundational lessons from the opinion writing block. If you skipped opinion writing, you should still teach the following lessons:

- Exploring Topics on page 14
- Narrowing Topics on page 17
- Researching an Opinion on page 20
- Writing a Thesis Statement on page 29
- Supporting Your Thesis on page 30

You should also skim through the rest of the lessons on opinion writing, including the optional lesson ideas, to see if there are any that your particular class might need to learn before proceeding with persuasion.

> Expectations for a Persuasive Essay

On page 51 you'll find a reproducible called *Expectations for a Persuasive Essay* that you should give to your students before beginning Step Three. This reproducible gives students a general idea of what will be expected of their finished persuasive essays. It is written in checklist format so that students can gauge the progress they are making toward the final product.

> The *Examining Persuasive Elements* Instructional Block

The purpose of Step Three is to get your young writers thinking about the elements of persuasive writing they'll need to understand before crafting their essays. They will think about their purpose, their audience, the validity of their evidence, and the evidence for the other side of their issue. When your students finish this block, they will be ready to begin drafting their essays.

This instructional block is based on a six-day schedule. Depending on the needs of your students, you may wish to extend some of the lessons over a longer period of time. You may also wish to teach some of the optional lessons (see page 69).

Each writing lesson has been paired with a recommended reading lesson. The six-day block in the following chart assumes that you have both a reading and a writing period in the same day. If you do not traditionally pair a reading lesson with a writing lesson, you'll need to adjust the block accordingly. To get the most out of the lessons, you should teach them in order. Note that I sometimes recommend that the reading lesson be taught before the writing lesson with which it is paired.

Day	Lesson Name	Description
Day 1: Writing	Author's Purpose in Persuasive Essays	Students will rewrite the informative topics of their opinion papers as persuasive topics.
Day 1: Reading	Comparing Informational and Persuasive Essays	Students will examine the similarities and differences between informational writing and persuasive writing.
Day 2: Writing	Understanding Audience (Day One)	Students will work on understanding audience and the effect of audience on writing style.
Day 2: Reading	Audience—Formal vs. Informal	Students will compare articles on the same subject written for difference audiences. They will examine the effects of audience on the formality of the writing.
Day 3: Writing	Understanding Audience—(Day Two)	Students will work on choosing an audience for their persuasive topic.
Day 3: Reading	Audience—Figuring out the Target Audience	Students will read articles and look for clues about who the intended audience is.
Day 4: Writing	Understanding Both Sides of the Issue	Students will work on deciding the pros and cons of their position.
Day 4: Reading	Further Research of the Pros and Cons	Students will work on finding research that supports both the pro and con side of the issue
Day 5: Reading	Relevant and Sufficient Evidence	Students will read persuasive articles and make evaluations as to the quality of the evidence presented.
Day 5: Writing	Criteria for Evidence	Students will examine their research and decide what evidence is relevant and sufficient for their persuasive essay.
Day 6: Writing	Discussing the Other Side	Students will think about the opposition point of view on their topic, and write arguments to rebut the other side.
Day 6: Reading	Revisiting Opinion Papers	Students will revisit their opinion pieces and read each other's work. As they read, they consider what arguments would have to be made to write an opposing opinion piece.

On page 69, you will find optional lesson ideas for Step Three. These lesson ideas, while optional, will assist your students in thinking about how they should and should not use evidence. Included are lessons in citing references, examining advertisements for proper use of evidence (including a reinforcement of the concept that evidence must be relevant and sufficient as discussed in Step Three, Lesson 5), and avoiding bias.

Expectations for a Persuasive Essay

After examining topics for your persuasive essay, choose one that you feel strongly about. Make sure you understand both sides of the issue before you begin drafting.

In your persuasive essay, be sure to:

- ✓ Introduce your essay with an interesting lead type.

- ✓ Include the five Ws to be sure you have fully explained your issue.

- ✓ Present at least three main arguments and discuss each in a separate paragraph. Support your argument with specific facts, quotes, and anecdotes that would appeal to your intended audience.

- ✓ Make sure that your evidence is relevant and sufficient.

- ✓ Address possible reader concerns, questions, and counterarguments by discussing both sides of the issue.

- ✓ Use several different paragraph types to appeal to your audience.

- ✓ Leave out unnecessary or inaccurate details.

- ✓ Conclude by using one of the closing types, and leave the reader with something to think about.

Remember to check your paper for proper spelling, grammar, punctuation, and paragraphing.

Lesson 1: Author's Purpose in Persuasive Essays

Why Teach It?

The purpose of many articles, advertisements, television shows, web sites, and books is to persuade.

Your students need to understand when they are being persuaded so that they can evaluate the validity of the arguments presented to them and make informed judgments. Reading persuasive pieces with a critical eye certainly helps, so it is an important part of this instructional block, but nothing makes students more conscious of the persuasive arguments of others than writing their own persuasive papers.

Focusing students on their purpose—to persuade—sets the goal for the entire instructional block. Every lesson that follows this one in some way echoes back to author's purpose. Teaching author's purpose at the start of the block helps students understand what they are going to be reading and writing about, and shows them the difference between opinion writing and persuasive writing.

In addition, being able to identify an author's purpose is a skill that is frequently assessed on standardized reading and writing tests.

Materials Needed

- Students' thesis statements from their opinion papers.
- The *Persuasive Writing: Author's Purpose* reproducible on page 54.

Opening the Lesson

Define *author's purpose* for your students as *the author's reason for writing what he or she writes.* Discuss with students the three main types of author's purpose: to entertain, to inform, and to persuade. Define each type if necessary, and elicit from students examples of each type from their reading. Explain that sometimes these purposes can overlap; for example, an informative piece can also be entertaining, but if the author's main focus was to give you information in an entertaining way, his *purpose* was still to inform.

Discuss the opinion paper your students completed in Step Two, and ask them what the author's purpose is when writing an opinion piece. While their papers certainly may have had entertaining or persuasive elements, they should be able to identify that their purpose was to inform. Discuss the differences between *informing* and *persuading*. You may want to have them copy the following, as it will help them truly understand the difference:

- In an opinion paper, your purpose is to inform the audience what you think about a topic.
- In a persuasive paper, your purpose is to convince that audience of what you want *them* to think about a topic.

You may wish to discuss how these goals differ before you move on.

Modeling the Skill

Explain that in their own opinion papers, each student had a purpose: to inform. You now want them to look at their opinion papers in a new way—given the information they've collected, what might they try to *persuade* their audience to do or think? Model this skill for them using an overhead of *Persuasive Writing: Author's Purpose* (see page 54). Use the thesis statement that you modeled for their opinion papers: *The cafeteria should serve healthier, better tasting food*. Write that statement in the thesis section of the overhead. Now brainstorm a possible persuasive topic for the class, such as *The cafeteria should make every Thursday a No-Fat Lunch Day*, *Students need a healthy buffet bar*, or *The lunchroom should serve vegetarian meals*. Ask students to help you brainstorm additional persuasive topics for this thesis statement. Create as long a list as you can.

Work Time

Tell students they are now going to work on this skill themselves. Give each student a copy of the *Persuasive Writing: Author's Purpose* reproducible. Remind them that when they created their previous topics, their purpose was to inform their audience. Now that their purpose has shifted to persuading their audience, their possible topics will change as well. Have them record as many possible persuasive topics as they can.

Closing Activity

Have students share their ideas. Because this is the first lesson for their persuasive papers, you may wish to take this opportunity to decorate your room with your students' ideas. One easy way to do this is to have students write their possible persuasive topics on chart paper in their groups. After they've shared their charts, you can hang them as decorations.

Recommended Reading Lesson: Comparing Informational and Persuasive Essays

Give students both an opinion piece and a persuasive article to read. Remind them that in the opinion piece, the author's main purpose is to inform, and in the persuasive piece, the author's main purpose is to persuade, or to change the way a reader thinks about a topic. Ask students to record any differences they notice between how the two pieces were written. If you wish, you can give them specific things to look for, such as titles, tone, examples used, sentence length, word choice, and so on.

An excellent resource for this reading lesson (and others in this book) is *Listen to This: Developing an Ear for Expository* by Marcia Freeman (Maupin House, 2003). This book contains sample essays, including persuasive and informational essays, for grade levels from 4-12.

Persuasive Writing: Author's Purpose

As we move from an opinion paper to a persuasive paper, your purpose changes from trying to *inform* your audience to trying to *persuade* them. Use your original thesis to create new persuasive topics.

In the center box, write the thesis statement for your original opinion paper. In each of the other boxes, write a possible topic for your new purpose: to persuade.

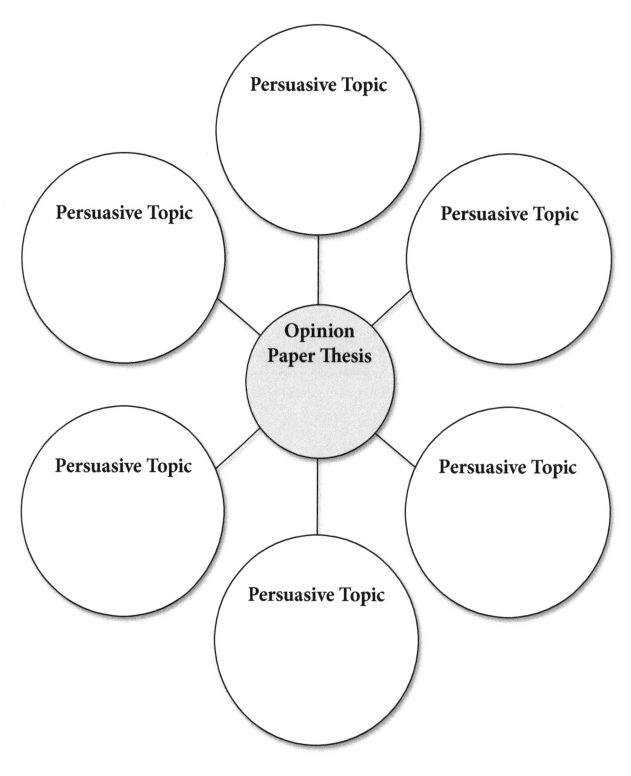

Lesson 2: Understanding Audience

Why Teach It?

It's important for students to learn that as their audience changes, so must their writing style and word choice. Persuasive writing is the perfect opportunity to teach them this valuable writing lesson.

This lesson is broken into two parts and should take place over two consecutive days. On the first day, students will concentrate on understanding what *audience* is and how their writing style will be affected by their choice of audience.

On the second day, the emphasis is placed on getting students to choose an audience outside of their immediate classroom. They may choose the principal or superintendent of schools, a coach, the city council, their senator, or some other person who has the authority to put their recommendations into effect. In addition, this lesson asks students to choose for their audience someone who may not necessarily agree with what they say. After all, that is the point of persuasion: if your audience already agrees with you, the entire argument is superfluous.

After choosing an appropriate audience, students will experiment with tone and word choice—elements of style critical to persuasion—when addressing that audience. This will give them a feel for what their persuasive essays should ultimately sound like.

Materials Needed

- The *Formal vs. Informal* reproducible on page 58 (for Day One).
- The *Choosing an Audience* reproducible on page 59 (for Day Two).

> Day One

Opening the Lesson

Define *audience* for your students as *the person or persons to whom a piece of writing is addressed.* Define *style* as *the tone of a piece of writing, as opposed to the content.* Add that style might include such things as word choice, sentence length, and even punctuation. Ask them to speculate on how a social studies textbook designed for an audience of second graders would differ for an audience from their own grade. When they are done responding, emphasize how audience affects style, and remind them that the audience they choose for their persuasive essays should affect the style they choose when writing them.

Modeling the Skill

Using either copies or an overhead of the *Formal vs. Informal* reproducible, read both paragraphs aloud with the class. Have them identify which paragraph is formal and which is informal. Ask them to identify the differences in style between the two paragraphs that helped them decide which paragraph was which. Prompt them if necessary to look for variations in word choice (vocabulary), sentence length, and punctuation. Ask them to speculate on the possible audience for each paragraph based upon the style.

Work Time

Have students create a writing notebook entry entitled *Formal/Informal Writing*. Give them the three prompts below, and ask them to choose one to work with. Instruct them that they should write two paragraphs for the prompt they choose—one formal and one informal. Tell them to write one paragraph as if they are addressing their best friend and one as if they are addressing the principal of the school. When they are finished with the paragraphs, ask them to reflect in their notebook on the choices they made for each audience. What were the differences between the two paragraphs?

- Write about the need for a shorter school day.
- Write about why you should be class president.
- Write about the need for more physical education periods.

Closing Activity

Ask students to share their paragraphs with their writing groups. Ask them to read both paragraphs to the group without revealing which is formal or informal. After each student reads, have the group decide which paragraph is which, and have students discuss the clues they used to figure it out.

> Day Two

Opening the Lesson

Write the phrase *Preaching to the Choir* on the board and ask students if they know what it means. Elicit responses, and then have them copy this definition into their notebooks: *trying to convince someone to believe something that they already believe.* Ask them to give you examples if they can. Then write down these examples and ask students to copy them:

- Trying to convince workers that they need more pay.
- Trying to convince students that they should do less homework.
- Trying to convince teenagers that they should have a car.

Tell students that none of these are appropriate audiences for a persuasive essay, as little or no persuasion is needed to get the audience to agree. Ask students to examine each example and change the audience so as not to preach to the choir. The first example might be changed to *trying to convince employers that their workers need more pay.*

Let students know that they should not be preaching to the choir in their persuasive essays, and that today they are going to choose appropriate audiences for their persuasive topics.

Modeling the Skill

Use an overhead to show students the *Choosing an Audience* reproducible from page 59. Show them how to fill in the chart by using an example like the one below:

What is the topic for your persuasive essay? Raising the minimum wage.

Who is the *choir* for this topic? Workers who earn the minimum wage.

Who is the intended audience for this topic? (Must NOT be someone "in the choir.") State senators.

List three things that will make this audience difficult to persuade:

1. They may see no need for higher wages.

2. Businesses will object to paying workers more.

3. The price of food and gas haven't gone up recently, so workers don't need more money.

Briefly list below some things you might have to discuss to persuade your intended audience: How much it costs to raise a family in your state, higher wages create more tax revenue, more workers will want to come to here so they can earn more, inflation has been greater than increases in the minimum wage.

Work Time

Give each student a copy of the *Choosing an Audience* reproducible and have them work on answering all the questions.

Closing Activity

Allow students to share their work. Some students may have difficulty answering all the questions, so allowing the group to give suggestions is helpful. Ask students to note any questions they had difficulty with, as you will explore this more in the next lesson.

> Recommended Reading Lessons

Day One: Audience—Formal vs. Informal

A great way to drive home the point about audience is to do a reading lesson comparing two articles on the same subject written for different audiences. Many newspapers and a few magazines have sections for children that discuss news items in kid-friendly language. Find an article on the same topic in the main newspaper, and ask students to compare them. Which seems more formal? How do they know?

Day Two: Audience—Figuring out the Target Audience

You can also ask students to read articles and to make educated guesses about the audience for whom the articles were intended. After they read, ask students to try to figure out the target audience of the article. Ask them to try to infer the gender, age, education level, and whatever other details they may be able to uncover. Have them explain their inferences.

Formal/Informal

Decide whether each paragraph is formal or informal. Write down the clues that helped you decide, such as word choice, sentence length, and punctuation

The lunches at this school stink! We definitely need better lunches, and fast. There's so much sugar in them! I get hyper for 30 minutes and then start snoozing in math class. They aren't healthy for you, either. After I eat, people can hear my stomach rumbling from a block away. I also put on about 10 pounds since coming to this school. I'm not eating any more than I used to, either.

_____Formal _____Informal

Clues you found:

....

The lunches at this school are definitely in need of improvement, and the sooner the better. For example, the lunches are so sugar-laden that students tend to get hyperactive for about thirty minutes, and then experience drowsiness by the time they get to their next class. There's nothing healthy about these lunches, if my stomach is to be believed. I frequently hear my stomach making rumbling noises for a significant period of time after eating. In addition, students complain of weight gain as a result of these unhealthy meals. I, myself, have gained ten pounds since the beginning of the school year without any significant increase in my food intake.

_____Formal _____Informal

Clues you found:

Choosing an Audience

What is the topic for your persuasive essay?

Who is the *choir* for this topic?

Who is the intended audience for this topic? (Must NOT be someone "in the choir")

List three things that will make this audience difficult to persuade:

    1.

    2.

    3.

Briefly list below some things you might have to discuss to persuade your intended audience:

Lesson 3: Understanding Both Sides of the Issue

Why Teach It?

If you had your students write an opinion piece prior to this persuasive piece, they should already have a fair amount of information about their topics. If not, it may be a good idea to teach Step One, Lesson 4 (see page 20) before continuing.

This lesson focuses on teaching students to understand both sides of the issue they have selected for their persuasive papers. This is often a difficult step for students because they most likely selected an issue they have strong feelings about and they may be reluctant to acknowledge that there is a legitimate opposing viewpoint.

Materials Needed

- The *Pros and Cons* reproducible on page 62.
- The *Choosing an Audience* assignment that students completed in Step Three, Lesson 2.
- Student research on their topics.

Opening the Lesson

Tell students that a persuasive paper must address reader concerns. When they selected an audience in Step Three, Lesson 2, they chose someone who is not a "choir member." Discuss how someone not in the choir may be unfamiliar with the topic and how they would likely want to hear both sides of the issues in order to feel informed. Discuss how writers need to convince their chosen audience why they should change viewpoints. To accomplish this, writers must show that they understand both sides of the issues they are arguing.

Modeling the Skill

Review the *Pros and Cons* reproducible (page 62) with your class. In the *Topic* space, write "School Uniforms." Remind students that part of persuasion is taking a position on the topic. Tell them that your position for this paper will be "Students should have to wear uniforms to school" and write that in the *Position* space. Then tell your students that in the *Pros* section, you're going to list some of the arguments in favor of your position. Your list may look like this:

Topic: School Uniforms
Position: Students should have to wear uniforms to school

PROS	CONS
Uniforms help create a sense of community in schools.	
Studies show uniforms decrease gang activity by banning "gang colors."	
Teachers don't have police student wardrobes.	
Security can easily identify people who don't belong in the school.	
Creates greater discipline in schools.	

After you have listed the "pros," ask your students to help you fill in the "cons" section.

Work Time

Distribute copies of the *Pros and Cons* reproducible and let students complete the handout using information about their own topic. Ask them to refer back to their previous research to help them fill in each box. Inform the class that they don't need to fill in every box, but they should begin thinking of what they *don't* know so that they can do further research.

Closing Activity

You may ask students to share their work to see if their writing group has any suggestions for filling in blanks. In addition, ask students to place a star next to any of their pros or cons that may require further research.

Recommended Reading Lesson: Further Research of the Pros and Cons

This is a great time to bring your students to the library or the computer lab for further research. They now know their position, and they should be more aware of the opposing side as well. They probably do not have statistics, charts, and quotes for all of the items on their *Pros and Cons* handout, so this is the perfect opportunity to allow them to research the items they placed a star next to in the writing activity.

Pros and Cons

Topic:_____

_____

Position: _____

_____

PROS	CONS

Lesson 4: Criteria for Evidence

Why Teach It?

This lesson will challenge your students to think about the quality of the information they have found in their research, and to make decisions about what they should include in their drafts.

Students will be asked to evaluate the evidence they hope to present in support of their position against two criteria: *relevance* and *sufficiency*.

Materials Needed

- Student research conducted in Step Three, Lesson 3.
- The *Criteria for Evidence* reproducible on page 65.

Opening the Lesson

Tell students that there is good evidence and bad evidence. Good evidence will be both *relevant* and *sufficient*. Have students discuss what those words mean. Then, you may wish to write the following definitions (from the *Merriam-Webster Online Dictionary*) on an overhead or on the chalk board for students to copy into their notebooks:

Relevant
Function: adjective
1 a : having significant and demonstrable bearing on the matter at hand **b :** affording evidence tending to prove or disprove the matter at issue or under discussion <*relevant* testimony>

Sufficient
Function: adjective
1 a : enough to meet the needs of a situation or a proposed end <*sufficient* provisions for a month>

Tell students they are going to practice determining whether evidence is relevant and sufficient, and then to apply that criteria to their own evidence.

Modeling the Skill

Use a transparency of the *Criteria for Evidence* reproducible on page 65 to help you model this skill.

Give students the following position statement: *Watching television causes violent behavior in children.* Fill in three of the boxes in the evidence column with the following "evidence" as follows:

Position: Watching television causes violent behavior in children.

EVIDENCE	RELEVANT?	SUFFICIENT?
After watching TV for about an hour, my little brother usually hits me on the head with his shoe.		
Households in the US have an average of three television set.		
A 2006 nationwide study showed an increase in violence among children who watched two or more hours of TV a day.		

Discuss each piece of evidence with your class. As you go, fill in the information for each box in the chart.

The first piece of evidence may have some relevance, because it is an example of the stated position. It is not, however, sufficient, because the behavior of one child proves little. It is impossible to generalize from a single example. Maybe his little brother just likes hitting people with shoes, or would hit people even without having watched TV.

The second piece of evidence isn't relevant to the topic. You should point out to students that if the evidence isn't relevant, it can't be sufficient, either.

The third piece of evidence is relevant because it deals directly addresses the position and the study is a recent one. It is also sufficient because the study is nationwide. Contrast this with the first piece of evidence.

In order to reinforce the concept of appropriate evidence, you should teach the Recommended Reading Lesson (see below) before continuing with the writing portion of this lesson.

Work Time

Give students a copy of the *Criteria for Evidence* reproducible (see page 65) and have them fill it in with evidence they've discovered in their research. Ask them to evaluate whether their evidence is relevant and sufficient and then to write their reasoning in the boxes provided.

Closing Activity

Because this can be a challenging activity, you should definitely have students share their charts and discuss their reasoning with the group. If disagreements about whether some evidence is relevant and sufficient occur, you may wish to ask students who disagree to state their cases, and let the class discuss their reasoning.

Recommended Reading Lesson: Relevant and Sufficient Evidence

Have your students read persuasive papers such as op-ed pieces and editorials. Ask them to evaluate the evidence they find. Encourage them to look specifically for evidence that does not meet the criteria of relevance and sufficiency. If they find any, ask them to speculate why they think the author may have used such evidence anyway. You may wish to give students a blank *Criteria for Evidence* handout sheet to fill in as they read.

Criteria for Evidence

Your position: _____

_____

EVIDENCE	RELEVANT?	SUFFICIENT?

Lesson 5: Discussing the Other Side

Why Teach It?

Discuss why it is important for persuasive writers to appear knowledgeable about the subject they are arguing. If the writer doesn't appear knowledgeable, why should the reader be convinced by her arguments? One of the best ways for a writer to show their credibility is to discuss both sides of the issue. Writers should anticipate the opposing side's arguments against their points and assure their audience that they have considered those arguments and were not convinced by them.

Fearing their inability to persuade readers with the strength of their own arguments, young writers frequently hesitate to mention the best arguments against them. Reassure your students that not addressing legitimate opposing viewpoints is not an option. If a writer doesn't address those, the reader will have the opportunity to question the bias and integrity of the entire essay. (You may want to do the optional lesson on avoiding bias—see page 69—if this is a problem for your students.)

Teaching students how to rebut the side of the argument that they support will also engage them in deep thought processes that can make their persuasive writing much more than more papers for their portfolios. Discussing the other side forces students to make judgments and to evaluate the merits of their own side of the issue. Students will be forced to rethink the strength of their own arguments and to select only those that best represent their side while refuting the opposition.

Materials Needed

- The *Discussing the Other Side* reproducible on page 68.
- The *Pros and Cons* handout your students completed in Step Three, Lesson 3.

Opening the Lesson

Remind students that one of the criteria for their persuasive essays is to *address readers' concerns by discussing both sides of the issue.* To do this, they will have to fully understand the arguments that the other side might make.

Modeling the Skill

Return to the *Pros and Cons* chart you modeled for the class in Step Three, Lesson 3.

Topic: School Uniforms
Position: Students should have to wear uniforms to school

PROS	CONS
Uniforms help create a sense of community in schools.	Might cost more money.
Studies show uniforms decrease gang activity by banning "gang colors."	Students lose their right to freedom of expression.
Teachers don't have police student wardrobes.	Students will be suspended for violations when they haven't done anything wrong.
Security can easily identify people who don't belong in the school.	Religious clothing might be prohibited.
Creates greater discipline in schools.	Uniforms aren't as comfortable.

First, have students evaluate whether the possible "Con" arguments meet the criteria for *relevance* and *sufficiency*. (These do to a greater or lesser extent.) Let students know that if an argument does not meet the criteria for evidence, there is little point in bothering to rebut it, and they should not include it as a possible argument for the other side.

Next, demonstrate for students how they might rebut each possible opposing argument.

Argument	Rebuttal
Might cost more money.	Uniforms generally cost less than the designer clothing many students now wear.
Students lose their right to freedom of expression.	Students can express themselves in other ways, perhaps with jewelry or hairstyles.
Students will be suspended for violations when they haven't done anything wrong.	The rules can allow for a "three strikes" policy before suspension.
Religious clothing might be prohibited.	An exception to the rules can be made for articles of religious clothing.
Uniforms aren't as comfortable.	Comfort is a small price to pay for safety and better discipline.

Work Time

Have students work on the *Discussing the Other Side* handout. They can fill out the *Argument* column directly from their *Pros and Cons* handout, as you modeled for them.

Closing Activity

Ask students to share their responses with their writing groups. After each group member reads, the rest of the group should comment on whether the rebuttal is as strong as or stronger than the original argument. If the rebuttal appears weak, it should be reconsidered and rewritten.

Recommended Reading Lesson: Revisiting Opinion Papers

This is a good time to have students revisit their opinion papers. Students can work as partners to read each other's work. As they read, ask them to list the arguments used in the paper. Then have them consider what counter-arguments they might use if they were to write an opposing opinion piece.

Discussing the Other Side

Argument	Rebuttal

> Optional Lesson Ideas: Adding Persausive Elements

Optional Lesson Idea A: References

Young writers often think that the information they find in books, encyclopedias, and especially on the Internet is in the public domain and available for everyone to use as they please without attribution. Because persuasive essays rely so heavily on researched facts as evidence, they present an excellent opportunity to teach students the difference between plagiarism and fair use of sources.

Have students create a bibliography page for their persuasive essays. Explain that their main purpose in creating a bibliography is to let the reader know exactly where the writer got his or her information, so it is important to write bibliographies in standardized forms. You may wish to show your students examples of how to cite books, magazines, encyclopedia articles, and even quotes from interviews so that they can give appropriate credit to their sources and avoid plagiarism.

Optional Lesson Idea B: Evidence in Advertisements

A fun way to show students how to examine evidence for relevance and sufficiency is to have them examine the advertisements in magazines and newspapers. By nature, these are almost always persuasive in some way. However, advertisements almost always fall far short of any reasonable standard of evidence. Challenge students to find ads that contain the least number of relevant and sufficient facts, and to evaluate the effectiveness of the ads. Ask students to explain how advertisers attempted to persuade their audience. What images and thoughts did the advertiser attempt to link to the product?

Ads by prescription drug companies are often good studies in contrasts, because pharmaceutical companies are required by law to list the negative effects of their products if they make any positive claims. Ask students to evaluate how drug companies emphasize the benefits of their products while minimizing their discussion of the risks.

Optional Lesson Idea C: Avoiding Bias

Explain to students that *bias is prejudice or favoritism to one's own point of view*. Since persuasive essays are supposed to present the evidence objectively, any perception of bias can lower a writer's credibility and should therefore be avoided. Nevertheless, it's quite difficult to write a persuasive essay without bias of some kind. Highlight this by having students read op-ed pieces by different authors on the same subject. Many newspapers now set up their op-ed pages with point/counterpoint style columns perfect for this purpose. Ask students to determine how each writer may have biased the information in his or her own favor. As they read, have students ask the following questions:

- What information did the author leave in or leave out?
- How does the author speak positively of his own point of view?
- How does the author speak negatively of the opposing point of view?
- Does the author ridicule the opposition in any way? If so, how?
- Does the author use mostly facts or mostly opinions?

After students have examined bias in the writing of others, have them survey the evidence in their own persuasive essays for signs of bias. Have them review the work they did in Step Three, Lesson 5 (see page 66) for signs of bias.

CHAPTER 5
Step Four—Crafting a Persuasive Essay

Writing a persuasive essay can be a formidable task for students, but in the end, it all comes down to mastering some basic writing-craft skills.

This chapter focuses on teaching students the Target Skills they will need to structure all their information and transform it into a cohesive essay.

Because persuasive writing is a more challenging genre to write than opinion, the lessons here offer skills for your students to use to get their positions across to the reader. Six different types of leads, closings, and body paragraphs are included. In addition, students will learn how to succinctly introduce the pertinent facts and arguments and to effectively present the opposing side without diminishing their own position.

It is particularly important to model these skills for your students when teaching the lessons in this chapter. Students must make quite a few writing decisions as they work toward completing their drafts, and it is necessary to model how to make those decisions. Each writing skill presented in this chapter is accompanied by a model to help you guide your class through the decision-making process.

> Expectations and Scoring Rubric for the Persuasive Essay

On page 73 you'll find a reproducible sheet of expectations to give your students before beginning work on Step Four. This sheet will give your students a general idea of what will be expected of them as they work through this instructional block. It is written in checklist format so that students can gauge the progress they are making toward their final products.

At the end of this chapter is a rubric that sets out exactly what your students will need to include in their persuasive papers (see page 104). It should be given out following the final lesson so that students know exactly how they will be graded before they begin writing the final copies of their drafts. The rubric is also helpful as a tool for peer editing, as students can evaluate each other using the same criteria you will use when you grade the papers.

Also available at the end of the chapter is a sample paper that you may share with your students (see page 105). Discuss it in terms of the rubric. It should rate a 3 or 4 in most criteria.

> The *Crafting a Persuasive Essay* Instructional Block

The purpose of this instructional block is to get your young writers thinking about how they will craft their persuasive essays. They will be asked to think about leads, closings, paragraph types, the Five Ws of non-fiction writing, and how to anticipate and refute opposing arguments.

The instructional block presented here is based on a ten-day schedule. Depending on the needs of your class, you may wish to extend some of the lessons over a longer period of time. You may need an additional day or two for actual drafting or peer editing.

Each writing lesson has been paired with a recommended reading lesson. The ten-day block in the following chart assumes that you have both a reading and a writing period in the same day. If you do not traditionally pair a reading lesson with a writing lesson, you'll need to adjust the block accordingly. To get the most out of the lessons, you should teach them in order. Note that I sometimes recommend that the reading lesson be taught before the writing lesson with which it is paired.

Day	Lesson Name	Description
Day 1: Reading	Examining Leads (Day One)	Students will skim their magazines and newspapers looking for effective lead types.
Day 1: Writing	Lead Types (Day One)	Students will examine several of the six lead types and write paragraphs for each one.
Day 2: Reading	Examining Leads (Day Two)	Students will skim for lead types and classify leads they find according to the six types they have learned about.
Day 2: Writing	Lead Types (Day Two)	Students will examine the remainder of the six lead types and write paragraphs for each one.
Day 3: Reading	Identifying the Five Ws	Students will read articles to identify the basic who, what, where, when, and why of each article.
Day 3: Writing	Writing about the Five Ws	Students will identify the who, what, where, when, and why of their persuasive essays an write a paragraph explaining them.
Day 4: Reading	Order of Importance Review	Students will read persuasive articles and determine whether the articles were written in order of importance or reverse order of importance. They will attempt to explain why the author made the choice he did.
Day 4: Writing	Organizing a Persuasive Essay	Students will write topic sentences and organize their facts in order to get ready to write their drafts.
Day 5: Writing	Persuasive Paragraph Types (Day One)	Students will examine several of the six persuasive paragraph types and write a paragraph for each one.
Day 5: Reading	Reading Drafts (Day One)	Students will read and evaluate the persuasive paragraphs written by their peers in today's writing lesson.

Day	Lesson Name	Description
Day 6: Writing	Persuasive Paragraph Types (Day Two)	Students will examine the remainder of the six persuasive paragraph types and write a paragraph for each one.
Day 6: Reading	Reading Drafts (Day Two)	Students will read and evaluate the persuasive paragraphs written by their peers in today's writing lesson.
Day 7: Reading	Reading Rebuttals	Students will read persuasive articles to see how authors deal with the opposing viewpoint.
Day 7: Writing	Including Opposing Facts	Students will learn two different methods of including opposing facts in their persuasive essays.
Day 8: Reading	Examining Closings (Day One)	Students will skim their magazines and newspapers looking for effective closing types.
Day 8: Writing	Closing Types (Day One)	Students will examine several of the six closing types and write paragraphs for each one.
Day 9: Writing	Closing Types (Day Two)	Students will examine the remainder of the six lead types and write paragraphs for each one.
Day 9: Reading	Examining Closings (Day Two)	Students will skim for closing types and classify them according to the six types they have learned about.

On page 101, you will find optional lesson ideas for this instructional block. These lessons, while optional, will assist your students in fine tuning their persuasive essays. Included are lessons on using quotes, statistics and anecdotes; avoiding logical fallacies; choosing persuasive words and phrases; and editing extraneous material.

Expectations for a Persuasive Essay

After examining topics for your persuasive essay, choose one that you feel strongly about as your topic. Make sure you understand both sides of the issue before you begin drafting.

In your persuasive essay, be sure to:

- ✓ Introduce your essay with an interesting lead type.

- ✓ Include the five Ws to be sure you have fully explained your issue.

- ✓ Present at least three main arguments and discuss each in a separate paragraph. Support your argument with specific facts, quotes, and anecdotes that would appeal to your intended audience.

- ✓ Make sure that your evidence is relevant and sufficient.

- ✓ Address possible reader concerns, questions, and counterarguments by discussing both sides of the issue.

- ✓ Use several different paragraph types to appeal to your audience.

- ✓ Leave out unnecessary or inaccurate details.

- ✓ Conclude by using one of the closing types, and leave the reader with something to think about.

Remember to check your paper for correct spelling, grammar, punctuation, and paragraphing.

Lesson 1: Lead Types

Why Teach It?

By now, everyone in your class should be brimming with information and ideas, but some students will inevitably stall out before they even begin because they simply don't know how to start their persuasive essays. For many students, the hardest part of any essay is the opening paragraph, or *lead*. By explicitly instructing your students in how to write various lead types, you not only help them get started on this paper but you give them a foundation for all future essays.

If your students began by writing the opinion paper from Steps One and Two, they already know one lead type—using an interesting fact or statistic. There are five more lead types discussed in this lesson, for a total of six. Your young writers will need time to read and construct a model paragraph for each lead type. For this reason, it is best to present this lesson over several days.

Materials Needed

- Copies of the *Lead Types* reproducible on pages 76-78.

Opening the Lesson

Remind students that a *hook* is designed to grab the reader's attention and drag them into the piece as if with a hook. Discuss the importance of an effective lead in getting the reader immediately involved with the essay. You may wish to ask students if they know any lead types.

Tell students that they are going to examine six different lead types and write a paragraph for each so that they can choose the one that best hooks the reader into their essay. Ask your students to create a page for each lead type in their notebooks before your begin. The six types you will examine together are

- An Interesting Fact
- A Question
- A Description
- An Anecdote
- A Quote
- A Bold Statement

Modeling the Skill

Give out the *Lead Types* reproducible (see pages 76-78). Choose which lead types you want your students to write each day. Read the descriptions of those lead types and the paragraphs themselves with your class. Discuss with the group how each lead type hooks the reader into reading more of the essay.

So your students can see how professional writers have used these techniques, you may wish to do the Recommended Reading Lesson below before continuing.

Work Time

After you've modeled the lead types and paragraphs you want your students to work on, let them spend their writing time crafting leads using the topic they have chosen for their persuasive essays. They should eventually write a paragraph demonstrating each lead type.

Closing Activity

As you circulate around the room during work time, look for good student-generated examples of each lead type. Ask those students to read their leads to the class. Have the class respond by discussing how the lead managed to hook the reader.

Recommended Reading Lesson: Examining Leads

Consider teaching this reading lesson at the start of each day that students are working on their leads.

Ask students to skim through their magazines and newspapers looking for the lead types you are working on that day. When they find one, ask them to note the source and page number so they can return to it easily. Ask students to read aloud any leads they found particularly interesting, and to identify the lead type the author used.

As a variation on this lesson, you may ask students to simply copy down any lead sentence they find interesting as they skim through their magazines and newspapers. When they are finished working with all the lead types, ask them to go back and classify those sentences according to the lead types they have learned. If they find a different or unusual lead type, you may want them to share it with their group or the class.

Lead Type 1—An Interesting Fact

When you use an interesting fact as your lead, try to choose something that your audience may not know but would be surprised to learn. Review your research to find the perfect fact. Open with the fact, briefly explain its significance, and then state your topic.

Position: We should pass a law mandating the neutering of pets.

Over five million dogs and cats will be issued a death sentence this year in our nation's animal shelters because there simply aren't enough homes for them. As tragic as that number is, it is doubly sad because not even one has to die. We must pass a law requiring all pet dogs and cats to be neutered until we can find homes for every animal on death row.

Lead Type 2—A Question

Starting with a question can be effective if the question causes the reader to begin to think about the issue. Avoid questions with simple answers, such as "Have you ever wondered whether women should be allowed to go to war?" because if the reader already has their mind made up, they may decide to read no further.

Position: Women should be allowed to fight in the military.

What might a war be like if half the soldiers were women? Some people believe that only men possess the bravery needed to defend their country, but there is ample evidence from other countries that allow women in combat that female soldiers are every bit as brave and effective as their male counterparts.

76

Lead Type 3—A Description

Using description gives your reader a way to experience something he may not have known or thought much about. Creating a negative or positive image at the beginning of your essay creates a mood for the reader that may help him to better understand your side of the issue.

Position: There is too much violence in video games.

A man stands in the middle of a crowded street holding a powerful automatic rifle. He looks left and right, trying to zero in on a target. One passerby seems to be a prime candidate for elimination. The man with the gun trains his scope on the passerby and squeezes the trigger. A boom that echoes throughout the town is heard and the victim barely has time to react before he is blown into a million fragments. This isn't a terrorist scenario—it is the latest video game that your 10 year old wants for his birthday.

Lead Type 4—An Anecdote

An anecdote is a brief story about an incident. It doesn't have to be a personal story; it can be a retelling of an event that you discovered in your research.

Position: You should be allowed to get cosmetic surgery as soon as you become a teenager.

After a sleepover at my cousin's house, I found her in the bathroom, looking into the mirror and sobbing uncontrollably. I asked her what was wrong, but all she could do was continue crying on my shoulder. Finally, she pointed to a bump on her nose that she had hated for years. The dentist had given her perfect teeth and the dermatologist had given her glowing skin. It made no sense that she couldn't legally go to a plastic surgeon and have that bump fixed until she was eighteen, but that is the law in our state. I believe the law should be changed so that people like my cousin can feel happy about themselves.

Lead Type 5—A Quote

Starting with a quote can be effective because it gives the reader the opinion of someone who is either an expert on the issue or who has had experience dealing with the issue. It is especially effective when the quote is either catchy or makes the reader think about what was said.

Position: We should abolish the death penalty.

"For centuries the death penalty, often accompanied by barbarous refinements, has been trying to hold crime in check; yet crime persists." That statement, as quoted in *The Columbia World of Quotations*, was made by Albert Camus, the famous philosopher and author, in 1961. It is as true today as it was when it was written. The death penalty was ineffective as a deterrent then, and it is equally ineffective now. It should be abolished once and for all.

Lead Type 6—A Bold Statement

Starting with a bold statement can "shock" the reader into reading on. These often take the form of "If/Then" statements, such as "If this doesn't happen, then that will happen." After you make your bold statement, back it up with a few brief facts that you intend to discuss more fully later on.

Position: We should enforce the death penalty.

If we don't start enforcing the death penalty soon, we can expect the murder rate to rise dramatically in our city within a few years. Last year alone, the murder rate rose 4.3%, which is the biggest jump and the highest rate in the last decade. Only if we keep our promise to execute murderers can law abiding citizens feel safe again on our streets.

Lesson 2: Writing about the Five Ws

Why Teach It?

The Five Ws—Who, What, When, Where, and Why—are crucial questions that students have to answer for almost any type of essay, including persuasive essays. For the student writer, understanding the Five Ws will help him get a grasp on the subject matter and explain it for the reader succinctly. For the reader, the Five Ws give the gist of the essay and explain what is to come.

In this lesson, students are taught the Five Ws by answering a series of questions and then writing the questions in paragraph form. This paragraph will become paragraph two of their persuasive essays, immediately after the lead paragraph. (If you wish, you can allow your more advanced writers to spread the Five Ws throughout the essay rather than place them in a single paragraph.)

Materials Needed

- Copies (and one overhead) of the *Five Ws of Persuasive Writing* reproducible on page 81.

Opening the Lesson

Explain to your students that the Five Ws are critical to many types of essays, including persuasive essays. In this lesson, they will answer the Who, What, When, Where, and Why of their persuasive essays and write a paragraph about them. Note that the Five Ws have been turned into questions that can be easily answered:

- Who is affected by this issue?
- What is the effect of this issue?
- Where is this an issue?
- When is this an issue?
- Why should the audience do something about this issue?

Modeling the Skill

Show the overhead of the *Five Ws of Persuasive Writing* to your class. Review the topic, position, questions and answers with the class. Note that *Why* should have at least three answers, since each body paragraph needs to include a reason why the audience should do something about the issue.

Read the model paragraph with your class. Point out how the answers to the Five Ws were used to form the paragraph. Ask students how the paragraph differs from the answers. They should be able to see that the paragraph sentences are not in the same order as the answers to the questions. Instead, the paragraph begins with the answers to the *Where* and *When* questions. Ask students to discuss whether this was a good choice or how they might have proceeded differently. In any case, students should be aware that they are not to simply string sentences together in the order of the questions, but they should think about how to best order their answers into an effective paragraph.

You may wish to do the Recommended Reading Lesson ("Identifying the Five Ws") before having your students continue with the writing portion of this lesson.

Work Time

Have students complete the *Five Ws of Persuasive Writing* (see page 81). They may write their paragraphs on the back of the page or in their notebooks.

Closing Activity

Ask students to switch papers with a partner. Have them read each other's paragraphs and identify each of the Five Ws. When they are done, ask them to justify their choice of sentence order to their partners.

Recommended Reading Lesson: Identifying the Five Ws

The Five Ws are a must for journalists, so a great way to work on this during your reading period is to have students examine newspaper articles. Ask them to read some articles and record the Five Ws for each article they read. Newspaper articles are generally not persuasive, so you may wish to modify the questions somewhat for this lesson so that they will apply to every article. Ask students to identify:

- What happened?
- Who did it happen to?
- Where did it happen?
- When did it happen?
- Why did it happen?

When students have examined a number of articles, ask them if any patterns begin to emerge. Which question gets answered first most frequently? Which next? Ask students to consider why these patterns exist, and why the pattern found in newspaper articles might not necessarily be the most effective for a persuasive essay.

The Five Ws of Persuasive Writing

Topic: Recycling
Position: We should pass laws making recycling mandatory.

- **Who is affected by this issue?** Everyone in our community and in the country.
- **What is the effect of this issue?** Lack of recycling causes pollution.
- **Where is this an issue?** All across America and in our own community.
- **When is this an issue?** Today, and for the past 10 years.
- **Why should the audience do something about this issue?** Recycling will keep our neighborhood cleaner, reduce greenhouse gasses, save energy, and reduce water and air pollution.

A lack of proper recycling has been a problem all across America and here in our very own town for the past 10 years. We are all affected by this problem because the lack of recycling pollutes our land and water. We need to start recycling now in order to keep our neighborhood cleaner, reduce greenhouse gasses, save energy, and reduce water and air pollution.

Topic:

Position:

- **Who is affected by this issue?**

- **What is the effect of this issue?**

- **Where is this an issue?**

- **When is this an issue?**

- **Why should the audience do something about this issue?**

(Write your paragraph on the other side of this paper or in your notebook.)

Lesson 3: Organizing a Persuasive Essay

Why Teach It?

If your students wrote opinion papers prior to working on this persuasive essay, they will be familiar with organizing the body of an essay. *Some* of the information and organization they used for their opinion pieces can be used for the persuasive paper, but the overall organization of a persuasive paper can be quite different. It will be longer, include more information, and will discuss the argument's opposing side.

When your students have completed this lesson, evaluate the results to see whether they included the interviews, quotes, and anecdotes they compiled while doing their research. If they did not, you should teach Optional Lesson A: Using Quotes, Statistics, and Anecdotes, on page 101.

Materials Needed

- All student research.
- The Model Organizer—*The Need to Recycle* on page 84.
- Copies of the *Organizing a Persuasive Essay* reproducible on page 85.

Opening the Lesson

Make sure each student has a copy of the *Organizing a Persuasive Essay* reproducible. You may wish to have a blank one on an overhead as you show the class how to use it. Ask students to identify some differences between the persuasive structure and the structure of an opinion paper. They may identify that it is longer, contains a position statement, addresses an audience, and answers the Five Ws.

Modeling the Skill

Tell the class to imagine that you are writing a persuasive essay on the need to recycle. Show them the model overhead on *The Need to Recycle*. Discuss your position and how your audience may influence your position. For example, the overhead says the audience is the city council. Ask how the essay might change it change if the audience were homeowners.

Next, show the class that the Topic, Audience, Position, Lead Type, and Five Ws have already been filled out. Have students fill out these spaces on their own blank organizers.

Tell students that when they wrote the *Why* section of their Five Ws paragraph, they basically listed their topics for their supporting body paragraphs. They can now transfer those to the topic slots on the organizer for each paragraph, and fill in the spaces for support with the information they've gathered during their research. Demonstrate how that was done using the model overhead.

You should do the Recommended Reading Lesson ("Order of Importance Review") before having your students continue with the writing portion of this lesson.

Work Time

Have students complete their graphic organizers using copies of the *Organizing a Persuasive Essay* reproducible. Let students know that they should have a minimum of three body paragraphs filled out. You should also inform them that they do not necessarily have to fill in all five of the support spaces for each paragraph, but if they have fewer than three, they should probably continue doing research to find more support for their topics.

Since they have not worked on closings yet, students should leave the "Closing Type" field on the last page of their organizer blank.

Closing Activity

Ask students to share their organizers with the group. If anyone is having difficulty, the group should assist in filling out the organizer.

Recommended Reading Lesson: Order of Importance Review

If you had your students write opinion papers, you may have already asked them to read articles for order of importance when you taught Step Two, Lesson 3: Organizing Your Information/ Finding a Clincher. If you didn't teach it then, you may wish to now. If you did teach it, you may want to revisit it now that you are working on organizing your persuasive piece.

Ask students to read persuasive essays and articles from their magazines or Op-Ed pieces from newspapers. When they have finished reading, have them record the main topics of the opinion piece. Ask them to decide whether they think the article was written in *order of importance* or *reverse order of importance,* and why they believe the author chose that form of organization.

Model Organizer—The Need to Recycle

TOPIC: Recycling
AUDIENCE: The City Council
POSITION: We should pass laws making recycling mandatory
LEAD TYPE: Bold Statement

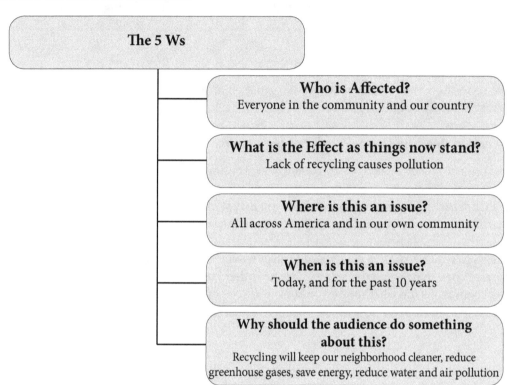

The 5 Ws

Who is Affected?
Everyone in the community and our country

What is the Effect as things now stand?
Lack of recycling causes pollution

Where is this an issue?
All across America and in our own community

When is this an issue?
Today, and for the past 10 years

Why should the audience do something about this?
Recycling will keep our neighborhood cleaner, reduce greenhouse gases, save energy, reduce water and air pollution

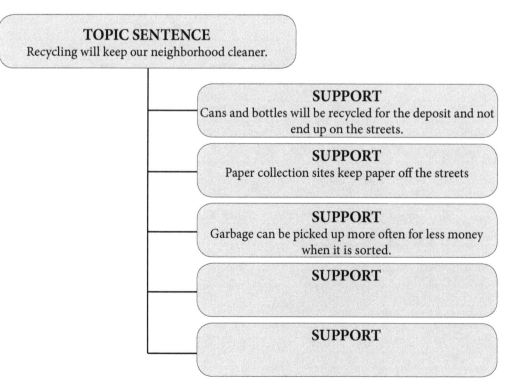

TOPIC SENTENCE
Recycling will keep our neighborhood cleaner.

SUPPORT
Cans and bottles will be recycled for the deposit and not end up on the streets.

SUPPORT
Paper collection sites keep paper off the streets

SUPPORT
Garbage can be picked up more often for less money when it is sorted.

SUPPORT

SUPPORT

Organizing a Persuasive Essay

TOPIC:

AUDIENCE:

POSITION:

LEAD TYPE:

The 5 Ws

Who is affected by this issue?

What is the effect of this issue?

Where is this an issue?

When is this an issue?

Why should the audience do something about this issue?

TOPIC SENTENCE

SUPPORT

SUPPORT

SUPPORT

SUPPORT

SUPPORT

Organizing a Persuasive Essay (continued)

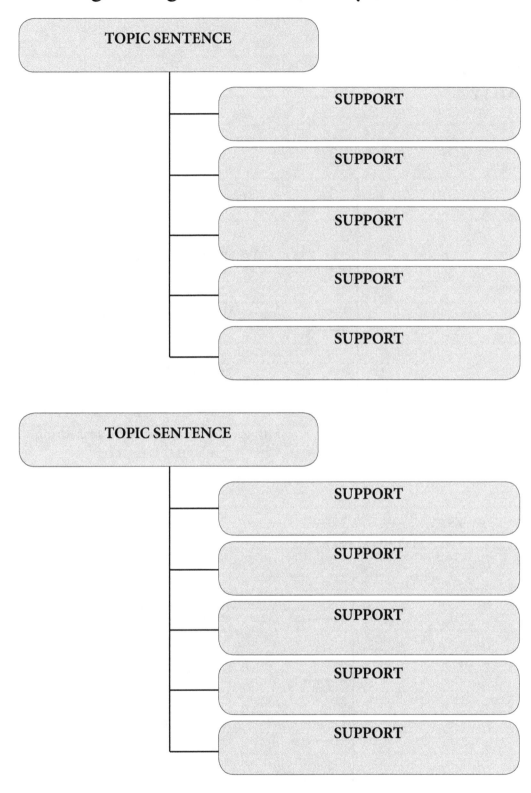

TOPIC SENTENCE

SUPPORT

SUPPORT

SUPPORT

SUPPORT

SUPPORT

TOPIC SENTENCE

SUPPORT

SUPPORT

SUPPORT

SUPPORT

SUPPORT

CLOSING TYPE:

Lesson 4: Persuasive Paragraph Types

Why Teach It?

For opinion papers (and for most student writing), paragraphs consist of a topic sentence and a number of supporting details. While students should be taught how to write such basic paragraphs, effective writing goes well beyond that simple format. Persuasive writing offers students an opportunity to learn a number of paragraph types that are extremely potent and convincing.

The paragraph types your students will be learning in this lesson are based upon arguments that appeal to the reader. There are six paragraph types here, so you may wish to present this lesson over a two- or three-day span so that your students will have time to examine each type and construct their own paragraphs based upon the models they will be reading.

Some of these paragraph types, such as *appeal to emotion*, can easily descend into logically fallacious arguments if they are not adequately supported by facts. You may wish to teach Optional Lesson Idea B: Avoiding Logical Fallacies on page 101 so that your students will understand the difference between a sound argument and a fallacious one.

Materials Needed

- Copies of the *Persuasive Paragraph Types* reproducible on pages 89-91.

Opening the Lesson

Ask students if they know what the word *appeal* means. Record various responses on the board or a chart. Then ask them what they think "appealing to the reader" might mean. Again, record responses.

Define those terms for students if necessary:

- *Appeal*: A plea for support or sympathy.
- *Appealing to the reader*: Writing in such a way as to get the support or sympathy of the reader.

Inform students that you are going to look at a number of paragraph types that are designed to appeal to the reader in different ways. They may decide to use some of these types when they draft the body of their persuasive essays.

Modeling the Skill

Give out the *Persuasive Paragraph Types* handout from pages 89-91. Choose which paragraph types you want your students to write each day. Read the descriptions of those paragraph types and the paragraphs themselves with your class. Discuss with the group how each type appeals to the reader.

Work Time

After you've modeled the paragraph types you want your students to work on, let them spend time crafting their own body paragraphs. Let students know that they are only experimenting and practicing during this drafting—they do not have to use all the paragraph types in their persuasive essays. Their purpose is to explore each type to see if it works with their particular topic.

Closing Activity

Ask for volunteers to read their paragraphs to the class. Have them read the paragraph without identifying the paragraph type. Ask the class whether they can identify the type used.

Recommended Reading Lesson: Reading Drafts

Have students share their drafts in their groups as a reading activity. Ask each student to read the draft paragraphs of every member of the group. They should read critically, and decide whether there is sufficient support for each topic sentence. They should also note whether any appeal made was effective. Students should place a sticky note with comments and questions on every draft they read.

Your class can continue this activity on another day if you intend to teach a two-day reading/writing block.

Persuasive Paragraph Types

Appeal to Logic. This is probably the most common type of paragraph, and one you're already familiar with. It is also the most effective, along with scientific or mathematical facts. When you appeal to logic, you give a series of facts, quotes, or other information along with a conclusion based on those claims. Basically, this means writing a paragraph with a topic sentence (the conclusion) and backing it up (supporting details). An appeal to logic often draws on some specialized knowledge that the audience does not have, such as information from your research. This is what distinguishes this type of paragraph from an appeal to common sense (see below).

POSITION: Motorcyclists should be forced to wear helmets by law.

About 5,000 motorcyclists were killed on the nation's highways last year. Yet many states have repealed their laws requiring riders to wear helmets. In those states that have repealed their laws, there has been an average increase of 30% in rider mortality. Ms. Lisa Petrowski, of the Highway and Helmet Association says, "Wearing a helmet is the single best thing riders can do to prevent serious injuries in the event of a crash." Given all this, it's clear that we should require all motorcyclists to wear a helmet whenever they ride.

Appeal to Common Sense. Common sense means good judgment. Usually, no special knowledge is needed for someone to use his common sense. It's common sense not to play catch with a bear you meet in the woods—you don't need to be a zoologist to know that bears can be dangerous. Similarly, if you can appeal to someone's common sense on your issue, you can often get him to agree with you.

POSITION: Every school needs a free breakfast program.

Every year, our teachers tell us to have a good breakfast before our state exams. They know that having something to eat before a test increases students' scores by as much as 10%. Before that big test day arrives, however, there are 120 days of learning in which being well fed is as important to a good education as it is on test day. It just makes sense to have a free breakfast program, so that every child has a better chance of success in school.

Persuasive Paragraph Types (continued)

Appeal to Shared Values. Values are beliefs that most people in a community or society have in common. For example, in democratic countries, most people believe in freedom, education for all, equal opportunity, and so on. A value can be any belief that you share with your audience. When you write an appeal to shared values paragraph, ask yourself what value you and your audience can agree on. Then explain how your position fits that value.

POSITION: Single parents should be allowed to adopt children.

Every child deserves a loving home. While we may disagree on what a traditional family looks like, we know that loving parenting makes a huge difference in the lives of children. Single parents can provide all the love a child needs, so why shouldn't single parents be allowed to adopt? Last year, 12 million families were one-parent households, so we know that single parents can be effective parents. By allowing singles to adopt, we'll create new, effective families with all the love an adopted child could ever want.

Appeal to Common Goals. A goal is a desired end result. Your goal may be to get good grades, go to college, or earn a million dollars by the time you are 25 years old. Your audience has goals, as well. If you can show your readers that accepting your position will result in them getting closer to or achieving their goal, you will have gone a long way toward convincing them to agree with you.

POSITION: We should take away the driver's license of anyone convicted of drunk driving.

We all want to make our highways and streets safe for both children and adults. Statistics show that almost half of us will be involved in an alcohol-related car accident in our lifetimes. Many of those accidents will result in injuries and fatalities. Therefore, making our highways safe will require us to take away the driver's license of anyone convicted of a DWI.

Persuasive Paragraph Types (continued)

Appeal to Benefits to the Audience. Before people take action, they often want to know what's in it for them. If you can convince your audience that adopting your position will be a benefit to them, you've gone a long way toward convincing them.

POSITION: We should build a new youth center in our town.

As a taxpayer, you may not want the expense of a new youth center. But think of it as a parent. A youth center that is open after school will give your child somewhere to go where he will be safe. Your child will have fun and still be supervised by caring adults. There will even be homework help in addition to all the sporting equipment to keep your child healthy and happy. And on Fridays, when the center is open late, you can leave your child there and sneak off to the movies without having to look for a babysitter!

Appeal to Emotion. If you can convince someone to feel happy, sad, or frightened about something, you can often get her to take action. Be careful as you write this paragraph, however, because appealing to emotion without using facts to back it up is a logical fallacy. A fallacy is a misleading or unsound argument. Sound arguments are backed by fact!

POSITION: We should hire more police.

Imagine walking down the street by yourself at night when you hear footsteps following you. You turn and see the glint of a knife. You look around for a police officer, but there are none to be found. This scenario is a reality for many people. Due to a 15% cutback in funding for the police department, there are far fewer officers on the streets at night. We need to hire more police before that nightmare scenario becomes a reality for even one more person.

Lesson 5: Including Opposing Facts

Why Teach It?

This lesson gives students the opportunity to do some real thinking about how they will structure their persuasive essays. They will see that good writers must make decisions at every step in the writing process.

Students will work on presenting the opposing facts to their arguments. They will work on presenting those facts in two ways: placed together in a single paragraph and spread throughout the body paragraphs. They will discover that both ways have potential benefits and drawbacks, but ultimately they will make the decision of which method is best for their own writing piece.

If you have done the optional lesson on avoiding bias (see page 69), remind students of that lesson and the need to present the opposing facts in a fair way. If you have not done that lesson, you may wish to briefly discuss what bias is and why it should be avoided.

Materials Needed

- Completed student copies of the *Pros and Cons* handout from Step Three, Lesson 3 on page 60.
- The *Including Opposing Facts* reproducible on pages 94-95.
- Sticky note pads.

Opening the Lesson

By now, students have drafted their leads and their body paragraphs. Let them know that it is now time to include the other side of the argument. Tell them that they can do this by writing a paragraph stating the opposing arguments or by spreading the opposing facts throughout their own body paragraphs. Let them know that neither is "better," and that they are going to need to try both methods to see which is the best choice for their piece.

Modeling the Skill

Remind students that when you began working on discussing the other side, you worked on the issue of school uniforms. Show them the *Including Opposing Facts* reproducible and read the Argument/Rebuttal chart with them to remind them of the arguments on both sides of the issue. Then show them how the three best arguments on the Rebuttal side now make up the Rebuttal Paragraph below the chart. Point out that writing a paragraph like this is one way they may present the opposing side. Ask what the potential plusses and minuses of presenting the information this way might be.

Next, show them the Body Paragraph 1 on the handout. This paragraph discusses the cost of school uniforms, but it only discusses one side. Model for students how you can add an opposing fact to that paragraph. Read Revision One and Revision Two with the class. Note that in the first paragraph, the opposing argument came early on, while it became the last sentence in Revision Two. Ask for opinions on which worked better and why.

So they can see how professional writers deal with opposing facts, you may want to have students do the Recommended Reading Lesson (below) before continuing with the writing potion of this lesson.

Work Time

Tell students that they are going to work on both ways of presenting opposing facts: first by writing a rebuttal paragraph stating the opposing arguments and then by spreading the opposing facts throughout their own body paragraphs.

Have students briefly review their completed *Pros and Cons* handout from Step Three, Lesson 3 on page 60. Tell them that they are to choose three arguments that state the opposing side's opinion and make a single paragraph out of them just as you did when you modeled the skill. Stress how they are rebutting each argument within one paragraph.

Then, ask them take out the body paragraphs they wrote in the previous lesson. For each of the body paragraphs, have students write a sentence stating and rebutting the opposition viewpoint on a sticky note. Tell them to place the sticky notes on their paragraphs exactly where they think the rebuttal sentences should appear.

Closing Activity

Students should share their work with their groups. Ask each student to read aloud to the group first their rebuttal paragraphs and then their body paragraphs with the sticky notes. Have the group offer opinions as to which method worked better.

Recommended Reading Lesson: Reading Rebuttals

Ask students to read some persuasive articles or op-ed pieces. As they read, they should examine how the author dealt with the opposing facts. Ask students to answer the following questions for each article:

- Title of Article or Op-ed piece:
- Author's Position:
- Opposing facts discussed:
- Method used to deal with opposing facts (single rebuttal paragraph or facts spread throughout the article):
- Explain why you think the method used was effective or ineffective:

Including Opposing Facts

Argument	Rebuttal
Might cost more money.	Uniforms generally cost less than the designer clothing many students now wear.
Students lose their right to freedom of expression.	Students can express themselves in other ways, perhaps with jewelry or hairstyles.
Students will be suspended for violations when they haven't done anything wrong.	The rules can allow for a "3 strikes" policy before suspension.
Religious clothing might be prohibited.	An exception to the rules can be made for articles of religious clothing.
Uniforms aren't as comfortable.	Comfort is a small price to pay for safety and better discipline.

REBUTTAL PARAGRAPH:

Those who oppose school uniforms often argue that they might cost more money, but uniforms generally cost less than the designer clothing that many students now wear. Opponents might also claim that students would lose their right to freedom of expression if they are forced to wear uniforms, but the truth is that students can express themselves in many other ways, including with hairstyles and jewelry. Finally, there is the fear that mandatory school uniforms might prohibit religious clothing from being worn. It would be easy, however, to include exemptions for religious clothing in the regulations. We would lose nothing by implementing a school uniform policy.

Including Opposing Facts

BODY PARAGRAPH:

One reason why we should implement a school uniform policy is cost. I priced school uniforms online, and I found that one week's worth of uniforms costs approximately $250. Another set of long sleeved winter uniforms would cost about $300 for five uniforms. In total, parents would have to spend about $550 for each child. I also found out that if the school orders the uniforms in bulk instead of parents ordering individually, the price drops dramatically. The cost then for both sets of uniforms would be only $400.

REVISION ONE:

One reason why we should implement a school uniform policy is cost. **While some might argue that uniforms are costly, I discovered that they actually cost far less than the designer clothes that most students now wear.** I priced school uniforms online, and I found that one week's worth of uniforms costs approximately $250. Another set of long sleeved winter uniforms would cost about $300 for five uniforms. In total, parents would have to spend about $550 for each child. I also found out that if the school orders the uniforms in bulk instead of parents ordering individually, the price drops dramatically. The cost then for both sets of uniforms would be only $400.

REVISION TWO:

One reason why we should implement a school uniform policy is cost. I priced school uniforms online, and I found that one week's worth of uniforms costs approximately $250. Another set of long-sleeved winter uniforms would cost about $300 for five uniforms. In total, parents would have to spend about $550 for each child. I also found out that if the school orders the uniforms in bulk instead of parents ordering individually, the price drops dramatically. The cost then for both sets of uniforms would be only $400. **So while some parents may be concerned that school uniforms will be costly, it's clear that they actually cost far less than the designer clothes that most students now wear.**

Lesson 6: Closing Types

Why Teach It?

Good closings are as important as good leads. However, by the time most students reach the end, they have often exhausted what they wanted to say. Their essays end abruptly or not at all. Teaching your students some closing types will assist them in finding the best way to leave a good impression on the reader.

There are a total of six closing types in this lesson. Students will need some time to read and examine a model paragraph for each closing type. Then they will write a paragraph for each type. For this reason, it is best to split this lesson over several days to give students a chance to really explore the various closing types they may choose from.

Materials Needed

- Copies of the *Closing Types* reproducible on pages 98-100.

Opening the Lesson

Discuss with students the idea that the purpose of their closing is not just to bring the essay to an end, but also to leave the reader with something to think about. Tell students that they are going to examine six different closing types and write a paragraph for each so that they can choose the one that best gives their essay a sense of closure and leaves the reader with something to ponder. You may wish to have students create a page for each closing type in their notebooks before your begin. The six types you will examine together are

- Writing a Summary
- Answering a Question
- Creating a Scenario
- Making a Recommendation
- Using a Quote
- Making a Prediction

Note that some closing types generally mesh well with certain lead types. Tell your students to keep their lead paragraphs in mind as they write their closings. If they began with a quote, closing with a quote may be effective. If they began by asking a question, then answering a question is a natural closing. This technique is called *circling back to the hook*. Some students may even change their minds about which openings they want to use when they start exploring closings.

Modeling the Skill

Give out copies of the *Closing Types* reproducible on pages 98-100. Choose which closing types you want your students to write each day. Read the descriptions of those closing types and the example paragraphs with your class. Discuss with the group how each closing type creates a sense of closure and leaves the reader with something to think about.

Notice that the Position statements for each model paragraph match the ones your students saw when they worked on lead types (see the *Lead Types* reproducible on pages 76-78). You may wish to have your class examine each closing in combination with the lead to decide whether they work together. The down side to doing this is that some students may feel that they *have* to pair certain leads with certain closings; make sure students understand that these pairings aren't the only acceptable ones.

So that students can see how professional writers have used these techniques, you may wish to have them do the Recommended Reading Lesson (below) before continuing with the writing portion of this lesson.

Work Time

After you've modeled the closing types and paragraphs you want your students to work on, let them spend their writing time crafting their own closings.

Closing Activity

As you circulate around the room during work time, look for good student-generated examples of each closing type. Ask those students to read their closing to the class. Have the class respond by discussing how the closing managed to leave the reader with something to think about.

Recommended Reading Lesson: Examining Closings

Consider teaching this reading lesson each day that students are working on writing their closings.

Ask students to skim through their magazines and newspapers looking for the closing types you are working on that day. When they find one, ask them to note the source and page number so they can return to it easily. At the end of the reading period, ask students to read aloud any closings they found particularly interesting, and to identify the closing type the author used.

As a variation on this lesson, you may ask students to simply copy down the final sentences of articles as they skim through their magazines and newspapers. When they are done, ask them to classify those sentences according to the six closing types they have learned. If they find a different or unusual closing type, you may want them to share it with their group or the class.

Closing Type 1—Writing a Summary

While a summary may not seem an exciting closing, it is often a good choice when the reader has been presented with a number of facts. Summarizing the information at the end of your essay gives the reader a chance to easily digest what you've written.

Position: We should pass a law mandating the neutering of pets.

In summary, remember that five million dogs and cats will die this year because of a lack of homes. That number has risen over the last few years, but we have an easy solution right at our fingertips. If we mandate the neutering of cats and dogs, we can make sure that there is a loving home for every stray animal. It's the least we can do for animals that give us so much joy.

Closing Type 2—Answering a Question

This is a great closing type to use if you asked a question as your lead type. Even if you used a different lead, you can pose a question to the reader and answer it in the same closing.

Position: Women should be allowed to fight in the military.

So what would it be like for women to fight in the military? We've read several examples of outstanding acts of bravery by women in the military. We've also seen the wonderful successes of other nations that chose not to discriminate against women in their armed services. I think we can assume that any female soldiers in our military would be more than capable of carrying on the proud tradition of bravery and service that has been a trademark of our fighting forces for hundreds of years.

Closing Type 3—Creating a Scenario

A scenario is a description of a possible future event. When you create this description, your goal is to get the reader to visualize what might happen if your position is ignored. If you describe it vividly enough, your reader will have that picture in his mind long after he has finished reading your essay.

Position: There is too much violence in video games.

So the next time you walk down a darkened street at night and you encounter a group of kids on a street corner, ask yourself: How many murders and acts of violence have they committed on their game console? Do they know the difference between reality and the fantasy of the gaming world? Do they understand that victims don't just get up and walk away like they do in video games? Think about it, and then walk past them, if you dare.

Closing Type 4—Making a Recommendation

You can create a great closing by using the body of your persuasive essay to point out the facts and then finishing with a recommendation of what to do based on those facts. Make sure that your recommendation makes sense based upon the information you've provided to your readers.

Position: You should be allowed to get cosmetic surgery as soon as you become a teenager.

While plastic surgery may not be for every teen, it is an ideal solution for some. Teens who want a new look should be guided toward counseling, and if they still want the surgery after a month of visits, they should be allowed to have it. In this way, we can ensure that it isn't a spur of the moment decision by an unhappy teenager but a well thought out plan that will bring happiness to a young heart.

Closing Type 5—Using a Quote

If you started with a quote, you may wish to end with the same quote and examine it again now that you've presented all of your information. If you used some other lead type, ending with a quote often gives your essay some authority by showing the reader that someone famous or an expert in the field agrees with your position.

Position: We should abolish the death penalty.

So as we've seen, the death penalty is simply not effective. It has little deterrent effect, it costs society a fortune, and the endless appeals process means that hardly anyone other than the poor ever get executed anyway. As Anna Quindlen said in *The New York Times* (as quoted in *The Columbia World of Quotations*), "Like cellulite creams or hair-loss tonics, capital punishment is one of those panaceas that isn't. Only it costs a whole lot more."

Closing Type 6—Making a Prediction

An excellent way to make your reader pause and think is to make a prediction about what will happen if your position is not followed. Unlike a scenario, which relies more on description, a prediction depends on your presentation of the facts. If your facts are well presented, the reader is more likely to accept your prediction as the possible outcome.

Position: We should enforce the death penalty.

We have seen the murder rate rise each year in this state since the death penalty was abolished. It is on track to rise again this year. If the courts are powerless to enforce the death penalty, it is only a matter of time before citizens take matters into their own hands. People like you and me will be forced to become vigilantes just to protect ourselves. The government should act now so ordinary citizen won't have to.

> Optional Lesson Ideas: Crafting a Persuasive Essay

Optional Lesson Idea A: Using Quotes, Statistics, and Anecdotes

Your students did a significant amount of research for their opinion papers and then their persuasive essays. Unfortunately, when students get to the drafting stage, they sometimes forget all the valuable information they actually have accumulated. It's common to see first drafts lacking any sort of quote, statistic or anecdote despite the fact that students often have collected such material.

One way to make sure such information gets into student drafts is to make sure they include it when they are working on organizing their essays. After they finish their handout from Step Four, Lesson 3: Organizing a Persuasive Essay, ask your students to place a star next to any quotes, statistics, and anecdotes they had included on their organizers. Ask them to count up the number of each type of evidence and to evaluate what they need to add to their organizers so that they have a wider variety of information types.

Optional Lesson Idea B: Avoiding Logical Fallacies

There are certain logical fallacies that tend to creep into student writing when they work on persuasive essays. While it is impossible to offer students an entire course on logic, you can easily show them the most common pitfalls and help students avoid them.

The best way to teach logical fallacies to young students is to give them lots of examples, and then ask them to come up with examples of their own. When they've got a handle on some of the fallacies they should watch out for, have them go through their papers and eliminate any fallacious arguments.

Here are some of the most common types, with examples:

ARGUMENTUM AD HOMINEM means an "argument to the man"; in other words, it is an attack against the person making the claim:

- Mr. Jones wants to eliminate the death penalty, but he's a criminal so of course he believes that.
- The principal wants school uniforms, but he's old and wants kids not to have any fun.

ARGUMENTUM AD POPULUM is an appeal to popularity. It claims a belief must be true because many people hold it:

- Most students in this school believe that we should have should abolish homework, so that must be the right position.
- Everyone agrees that punishing criminals for a long time is a way to fight crime effectively.

HASTY GENERALIZATION is using a small sample to represent the whole. The generalization *might* be true, but the sample is too small to prove it:

- Neither of my best friends likes the school lunch, so obviously everyone hates it.
- I was adopted and I'm very happy, so adoption is always a wonderful thing for children.

SLIPPERY SLOPE is claiming, without any evidence, that one event will lead to another:

- If we let the government take away guns, next thing you know they'll take away all our freedoms!
- If everyone has a gun, crime will spiral out of control.

POST HOC comes from the Latin "post hoc ergo propter hoc," and means "after this, therefore because of this." A post hoc argument says that because one thing happened before a second thing, it is the cause of the second thing. Correlation is not proof of cause:

- Most people die in their sleep, so it is not a good idea to sleep.
- After the school budget went up, test scores went down, so money does more harm than good.
- Our school had few suspensions before we got a dean, so getting rid of the dean will mean better student behavior.

Optional Lesson Idea C: Choosing Persuasive Words and Phrases

Certain words and phrases lend themselves naturally to persuasive writing. Using a student draft as a model, show students how they can improve their writing through careful selection of some of the phrases below:

- **Words and phrases to use in the Lead:** I believe, in my opinion, in my experience, it is obvious (certain, clear) that, it is my position that.
- **Words and phrases to use in the Body:** First, second, third, finally, lastly, additionally, for example, in fact, in truth, in reality, furthermore, again, moreover, therefore, nevertheless, in spite of, despite, on the contrary, since, as a result, because of, in consequence of, essentially, accordingly, it is commonly held that, on the other hand, in contrast, in like manner, similarly, however.
- **Words and phrases to use in the Closing:** Finally, lastly, most importantly, in conclusion, in summation, in brief, as you can see, for all these reasons, without question, beyond all question, clearly, obviously, we must conclude that, there is no doubt that, without a doubt.

After you have modeled the skill, ask students to go through their own leads, closings, and body paragraphs and to make changes that improve the quality of their writing.

Optional Lesson Idea D: Editing Extraneous Material

One of the essentials of persuasive writing is that the arguments and discussions be free of unnecessary information. Students need to make sure they are focused on the topic at hand. After they have drafted, teach a mini-lesson about editing extraneous material from their work. Explain that *extraneous* simply means that something is "extra" because it does not belong. Give students sample paragraphs like the one below as practice. Ask them to identify any extraneous sentences. When they are done with the practice, have them review their own drafts and delete any irrelevant sentences.

SAMPLE PARAGRAPH: We need to hire more sanitation workers to help keep our city clean. Last year, we lost 5% of the sanitation force to retirement. My uncle retired from his job as a policeman, too. Because we lost so many workers, garbage is piling up on our streets. Littering is illegal, so why do people do it? Anyway, piles of garbage are now on our streets, and this is attracting all sorts of pests, such as bugs and rats. Rats are yucky, but I had a cute one as a pet when I was younger. These pests can bring all sorts of disease to our city. I hate being sick. If we don't correct this situation, our city may end up looking like a garbage dump.

Rubric for a Persuasive Essay

IN YOUR PERSUASIVE ESSAY, DID YOU:	OUTSTANDING 4	GOOD 3	NEEDS IMPROVEMENT 2	NOT DONE 1
Begin with an engaging introduction using an interesting lead type?	Thoroughly engages the reader. Lead type is perfectly suited for the topic.	Engages the reader in the topic. Lead type is appropriate for the topic.	Introduction does not truly engage the reader or the lead type is inappropriate for the topic.	Little attempt to engage the reader or use one of the lead types.
Present at least three main arguments and support them with specific facts, quotes, and anecdotes that appeal to the intended audience?	Supports each argument with a wide variety of appropriate information that will appeal to the intended audience.	Supports each argument with a good amount of appropriate information, much of which will appeal to the intended audience.	Presents three arguments, but fails to support them adequately through use of a variety of information. May not appeal to the intended audience.	Fewer than three arguments or the arguments are not supported well. Fails to appeal to the intended audience.
Include the five Ws of non-fiction writing?	Uses the Five Ws to effectively discuss the facts of the topic.	Uses the Five Ws to discuss the facts of the topic.	The Five Ws are generally present and clear.	Some or all of the Five Ws are missing.
Use relevant and sufficient evidence?	All evidence is relevant and sufficient.	Most evidence is relevant and sufficient.	Some evidence is relevant and sufficient.	Little if any evidence is relevant and sufficient.
Address possible reader concerns, questions, and counterarguments by discussing both sides of the issue?	Fully addresses possible reader concerns, questions, and counterarguments by discussing both sides of the issue.	Mostly addresses possible reader concerns, questions, and counterarguments by discussing both sides of the issue.	Occasionally addresses possible reader concerns, questions, and counterarguments by discussing both sides of the issue.	No attempt to address possible reader concerns, questions, and counterarguments by discussing both sides of the issue.
Include several different paragraph types to appeal to your audience?	A great mix of paragraph types that appeal to the reader.	A good mix of paragraph types that appeal to the reader.	Essay would benefit from more paragraph types that appeal to the reader.	Little use of different paragraph types.
Leave out unnecessary or inaccurate details?	All details are necessary and accurate. Details support the arguments made.	Most details are necessary and accurate. Details mostly support the arguments made.	Some details may be unnecessary or inaccurate.	Contains unnecessary or inaccurate details.
Conclude by using one of the closing types, and leave the reader with something to think about?	Great choice of closing type. Leaves the reader with a new perspective on the issue.	Good choice of closing type. Leaves the reader with something to think about.	May not be the perfect closing type for this essay, or leaves the reader with little to think about.	No real attempt made to close properly or to leave the reader with something to think about.

COMMENTS:

Gold Garbage

Garbage can be beautiful! Well, maybe not beautiful, but instead of looking at tattered newspapers, crumpled aluminum cans, and old tires as ugly junk, we should be looking at items like these, that can be recycled, as valuable resources that should be cultivated and harvested. We should pass laws making recycling mandatory.

A lack of proper recycling has been a problem all across America and here in our town for the past 10 years. We are all affected by this problem because the lack of recycling pollutes our land and water. We need to start recycling now in order to keep our neighborhood cleaner, reduce greenhouse gasses, save energy, and reduce water and air pollution.

Recycling will keep our neighborhoods cleaner. Trash that is not recycled often ends up on our streets. If we made recycling mandatory, people would turn in their cans and bottles instead of throwing them on the ground. On busy city sidewalks where paper recycling bins are placed every fifty feet, loose paper trash declines by 85%. With weekly pickup of recyclables from homes, many plastics, metals, and papers could be recycled instead of ending up on sidewalks, ponds, and roadways. With a mandatory recycling law, the increased cleanliness would lead to more people taking pride on our city's appearance.

On Earth Day last year, Mayor Edelstine said that everyone should make an effort to reduce greenhouse gasses. Mandatory recycling would reduce greenhouse gasses in many ways. For instance, by recycling and reusing resources like the aluminum from drink cans, we would not need to make as much new aluminum, which would save the greenhouse gasses normally emitted in the process. Also, the more paper we recycle, the fewer trees need to be cut down every year. Trees absorb greenhouse gasses. A law making recycling mandatory would show that the city council was listening to the mayor.

An article I read in *Environment Extras!* pointed out that almost 35% of all greenhouse gasses are emitted while gathering the raw materials needed for the manufacturing process. Additionally, gathering raw materials is responsible for almost 60% of air and water pollution. Mandatory recycling laws would make using recycled materials easier and cheaper, meaning they will be used more in the production process. This would obviously have a huge impact on pollution and the production of greenhouse gasses.

Critics say that a mandatory recycling law would be too expensive to enact. Mr. Edwards at the city planning office confirmed that such a law would be expensive at first. The city would have to construct and install appropriate collection bins in convenient places. We would need to buy two new trucks to handle the sorted loads and increased volume. We would need to hire five additional workers to manage the process. However, Mr. Edwards told me that we would be able to market our recycled materials to manufacturers around the country. We would also be able to offer sorting and extraction services to surrounding cities. This income would pay for the initial costs in five to eight years. Within twenty years, the program could actually pay for city-wide tax cuts.

So the next time you walk down the street, look at the trash lining the gutters and sidewalks. Ask yourself if the image of crushed cans and loose newspapers is the one we want connected to our city. Then picture recycling bins where the trash currently sits. Imagine our city not as a dumping ground but as a sparkling clean leader in the recycling industry. Picture the new jobs a recycling industry would bring to our town. Finally, imagine the children of tomorrow playing in a clean city and thanking you for passing mandatory recycling laws today.

Bibliography

Clifford, Tim. *The Middle School Writing Toolkit*. Gainesville, FL: Maupin House, 2006.

Freeman, Marcia. *Crafting Comparison Papers*. Gainesville, FL: Maupin House, 2006.

Freeman, Marcia. *CraftPlus K-8 Writing Program and Professional Development Resource*. Gainesville, FL: Maupin House, 2003.

Koehler, Susan. *Crafting Expository Papers*. Gainesville, FL: Maupin House, 2007.

Merriam-Webster Online Dictionary. 2007. http://www.merriam-webster.com. (7 Jan. 2007).

The Columbia World of Quotations. New York: Columbia University Press, 1996. www.bartleby.com/66/. (28 Jul. 2006).

Wilhelm, J. D., Baker, T. N., & Dube, J. *Strategic Reading: Guiding Students to Lifelong Literacy*. Portsmouth, NH: Heinemann, 2001.

APPENDIX:

A Brief Overview of the CraftPlus® Curriculum

by Susan Koehler

The teaching methods and concepts presented in this book are based on the principles and practices of CraftPlus®, an approach to writing instruction that was developed by Marcia S. Freeman.

CraftPlus instruction is a curriculum built upon the explicit teaching of writing craft, presented as isolated Target Skills®. Target Skills® are modeled and directly taught. Students are provided with ample practice and support as they develop facility with Target Skills. The ultimate goal is for students to apply these writing-craft skills competently and creatively in their written work.

> CraftPlus Principles

- The writing process is what writers *do*; writing craft is what writers *know*.
- Writing craft is a set of specific organizational, composing and convention skills.
- Writing should be viewed as an academic subject that is explicitly taught.
- Like all effective teaching, writing-craft instruction should proceed from simple to complex, and from concrete to abstract.
- CraftPlus emphasizes non-fiction, which encompasses most of our required writing.
- CraftPlus links writing to reading with the use of literature models, which builds and reinforces both language processes.

> CraftPlus Practices

- Lessons are focused on specific Target Skills.
- Writing is taught using models from printed works and student writing.
- Composing and convention skills are applied across genres.
- Organizational strategies are taught as genre-specific processes.
- Genre-specific writing-craft skills are taught and applied in genre blocks.
- Student writing assignments consist of 85% practice and 15% assessment.
- Writing instruction is conducted in a daily writing workshop environment tied to short, focused mini-lessons.
- Traditional writing process strategies are modified to include procedures for peer response, revision and editing.
- Revision is emphasized. Teaching with Target Skills gives students specific revision goals.
- Student writers maintain personal writers' notebooks. Teachers maintain instructional notebooks or files.
- Writing assessment is objective, focusing on specific organizational, composing, or convention skills.

> A Sample of Target Skills

Organizational

listing	sorting/classifying	ordering
transitions	graphic organizers	establishing focus
beginning techniques	ending techniques	paragraph structures

Composing

specificity	voice	supporting detail types
dialogue	clues for inference	literary devices

Conventions

punctuation	capitalization	grammar

> Methodology

CraftPlus lessons are based on teaching craft through Target Skills and modeling. Lessons generally follow this sequence:

- Expose students to a new Target Skill by using a literature model.
- Discuss the skill or technique.
- Model the use of the skill, both orally and in writing.
- Allow students to practice the skill, first orally and then in writing.
- Provide opportunities for practice with lots of encouragement and feedback, along with supplementary modeling and instruction.
- Finally, assess students' mastery of the Target Skill in a required written piece.

> Lesson Plans

Teachers who implement the CraftPlus curriculum maintain instructional notebooks or files, which continue to grow from year to year with additional lesson plans, models, assessment options and teaching ideas.

A lesson plan follows this general order:

1. Objective (Target Skill)
2. Genres to which the Target Skill can be applied
3. Time parameters
4. Materials
5. Literature models
6. Procedure: Mini-lesson, Workshop, Response, Follow-up lessons

> Models

Target Skills should always be presented in models. Models can be collected from literature, textbooks, magazines, student work, and teacher composition.

Models should be brief, focused and well-crafted. If you wish to model a non-example (a poor application) of a Target Skill, create that model yourself. Never use a student's work as a non-example.

Save models in your writing instruction notebook or files. As years go by, your resources will grow.

> Genre Blocks

A genre block is a period of time you devote to instruction in a specific genre. This book presents lessons for a thorough expository genre block. Over the course of the genre block, skills are explicitly taught and practiced.

Select skills from each set: organizational, composing and conventions. Students in fourth through tenth grades can handle several Target Skills during a genre block. Some skills are usually review skills, while others are new skills.

After teaching the set of skills you have designed for any genre block, plan a writing piece which requires students to apply those skills. During the last few days of the genre block, provide instruction in revising and editing. Allow students to practice these skills as they polish and refine their composition.

> Assessment

Because Target Skills are focused and specific, assessment can be objective. Use a single-skill rubric for assessing mastery of a single Target Skill. Use the multiple-skill assessment rubric for assessing multiple Target Skills or a genre-block writing piece. If you need to attain a percentage, you can use a weighted checklist for assessing a writing piece.

No matter which instrument you use, assessing Target Skills should be directly tied to instruction. Use assessments to evaluate mastery and determine specific needs for re-teaching and remediation.

> Remember

CraftPlus principles are consistent with current educational theory and practice. Instruction is direct and explicit. Modeling is at the heart of instruction. Skills are taught in a systematic manner, progressing from simple to complex and from concrete to abstract.

Students are provided with ample practice and assessment is authentic and tied to instruction. The curriculum emphasizes non-fiction writing, which accounts for the bulk of writing that will be required of students in their adult and professional lives.